PAST PRESENT

MONTEVALLO

OPPOSITE: Main Hall, the largest dormitory on campus, was constructed sequentially with three wings named after early faculty members Elizabeth Haley, Anne E. Kennedy, and Mary Goode Stallworth between 1897 and 1908. This c. 1900 photograph taken beside the Haley wing shows workers preparing mud for bricks as the horse would pull the wheel in a circle mixing the "batter" that would form the eventual bricks. (Courtesy of the Anna Crawford Milner Archives and Special Collections.)

PAST & PRESENT

MONTEVALLO

Carey W. Heatherly and Clark Hultquist

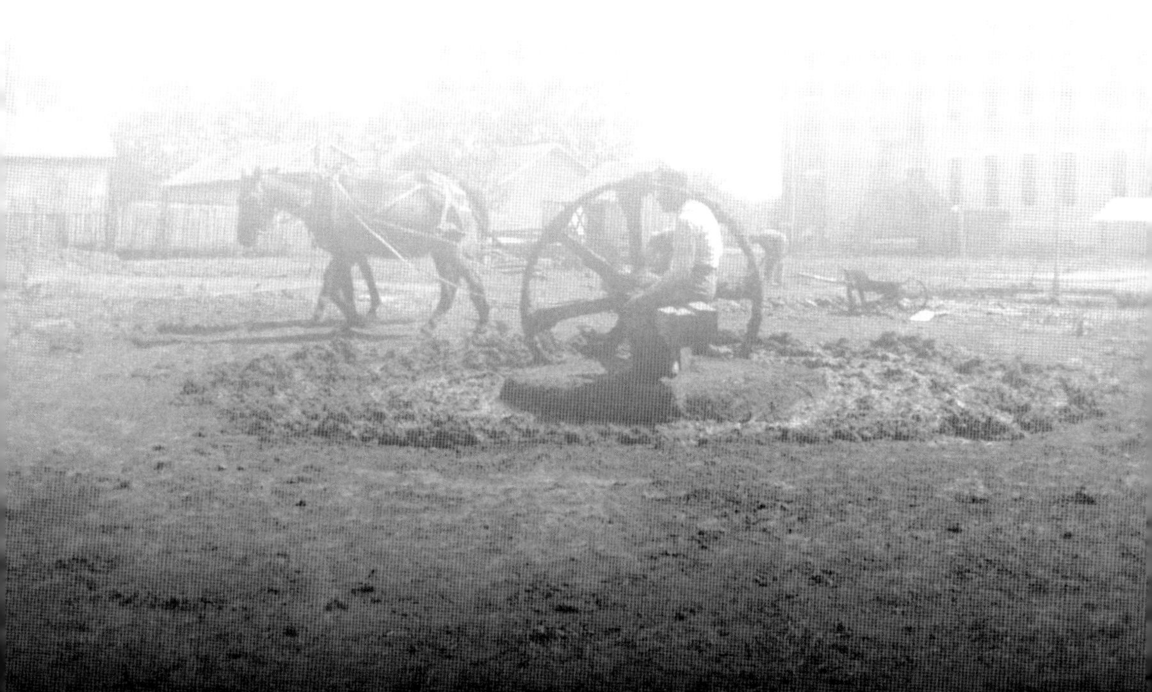

For my girls: Mandy, Ava, Celia, and Eliza

—Carey

For my mother, my brothers, and my sisters

—Clark

ISBN 978-1-4671-6098-8

Library of Congress Control Number: 2023948076

Published by Arcadia Publishing
Charleston, South Carolina

Printed in the United States of America

For all general information, please contact Arcadia Publishing:
Telephone 843-853-2070
Fax 843-853-0044
E-mail sales@arcadiapublishing.com

Visit us on the Internet at www.arcadiapublishing.com

On the Front Cover: Reynolds Hall (built in 1851) first served as an academy for boys and later added girls in 1858. After the Civil War, the structure intermittently operated as a school until it became the cornerstone of the Alabama Girls' Industrial School in 1896. Reynolds Hall long housed the university theater and classroom space and currently is the home for alumni affairs, admissions, and esports. (Past image courtesy of the Anna Crawford Milner Archives and Special Collections; present photograph by Clark Hultquist.)

On the Back Cover: One of the most beautiful buildings on campus, the Colonial Williamsburg–style Calkins Hall served as home to the Department of Music from 1917 to 1971. The building included a small concert hall and numerous decorative motifs of musical instruments. This 1980s photograph shows the building in its current use for university administration, including the offices of the president and the provost. (Courtesy of the Anna Crawford Milner Archives and Special Collections.)

Contents

ACKNOWLEDGMENTS

In the 20 months of research and writing of this book, many individuals and institutions have afforded us generous assistance. This work would not be possible without them.

We are grateful for the assistance of Clay Nordan, the late H.G. McGaughy, Janice Burks, Billy Hughes, Dee Woodham, Charlotte Ford, Ruth Smith Truss, Jim and René Day, Joel Bullock, Kira Thomas, Alyssa Luna Green, Kathy King, Melanie Poole, Jamal Rasheed, Mikayla Shannon, Raegan Lindsay, Kristen Standlee, Delaney Williams, Beverly Stamps, Mark Robinson, Henry Emfinger, Rod Hildreth, David Hodnett, Stacia Brady, Meredith Tetloff, Andrea Eckelman, Rachel Jubran, Marty Everse, Howard Stanger, J. Ross McCain, the Shoal Creek Park Foundation Board, Montevallo Historical Society, and the Alabama Department of Archives and History.

We are most thankful for the guidance afforded to us by Arcadia Publishing and its professional staff, including Amy Jarvis, Lindsey Givens, and Steve Sawyer.

Unless otherwise noted, all past images appear courtesy of the Anna Crawford Milner Archives and Special Collections at the University of Montevallo. All present images are courtesy of Clark Hultquist.

INTRODUCTION

In 2017, the city of Montevallo celebrated its bicentennial. Over the last 200 years, a small village near the exact center of the state has grown and prospered into a city of over 7,000 people. Since 1896, it has been a college town with all the requisite connotations of a city somewhat bifurcated into what is described as "town and gown"—two opposed worlds of a college population and the local residents. Over this period of time, relations between the two areas have been reasonably civil, with a number of local residents (or their children) attending the school and many university members either living in town or participating in local politics. Certainly, neither entity could exist without the other.

One could periodize Montevallo's history since 1817 in a few phases: early settlers and a plantation era up to 1865; mining and the growth of natural resource extraction, including timber, from 1865 to the 1940s; and finally, the rise of the service sector from the 1950s to the present. All of this is overlaid by various types of secondary schools from the 1850s on and the 1896 establishment of the Alabama Girls' Industrial School. Montevallo's prime central location, easy access to Birmingham, and powerful legislative interests saw the city host the school, the predecessor to Alabama College and the University of Montevallo. Birmingham, the so-called "Magic City" some 30 miles north, was entering a boom era and needed educated women for new jobs. The State of Alabama began to expand primary education, and a host of teachers were necessary for the modernizing economy. The combination of these forces ensured the school's early enrollment success.

The original central core of the town was laid out in the 1820s in a symmetrical grid pattern in hopes of luring what was to be the University of Alabama. Although this effort failed, the end result is still evident in a 10-square-block area. A few late Victorian homes still grace the city, though many finer structures were razed during the 20th century. While many smaller towns in the United States are facing population crises, with the requisite boarded-up windows and empty storefronts, Montevallo has escaped this trend with a combination of good leadership, demographic changes, and socio-economic development in Shelby County, one of the fastest-growing counties in the state. A $2.3-million grant from the Alabama Department of Transportation along with local matching funds allowed an overhaul of downtown with new traffic signals, parking, and ADA (Americans with Disabilities Act)–compliant sidewalks. In 2020, Montevallo earned an Accredited Main Street America Program, which acknowledged the town's commitment to downtown revitalization.

The metropolitan Montevallo area enjoys varied environmental assets. Besides the coal, lime, and timber resources, the city has ample water supply via Spring Creek and Shoal Creek, the latter of which meanders through town. The name *Montevallo* means "mountain in a valley," and while no real mountain is present, the city does have rolling features as it sits on a plateau above outlying areas. Local waterfalls like Davis Falls and Falling Rock are just a few miles from downtown, as is Ebenezer Swamp, an ecological preserve owned by the university. Three major parks—Orr Park, Shoal Creek Park, and Stephens Park—allow hiking, walking, baseball, and places for natural observation and reflection. A loop trail connects Orr Park to Stephens Park.

As for the university in this period, the Alabama Girls' Industrial School eventually became Alabama College, the State College for Women, in 1923. Soon after, the school gained four-year accreditation, and its president, Oliver Cromwell Carmichael, envisioned a much larger college than its then-600 students. As a result, the school's layout and development changed with a "Million Dollar Drive" campaign launched in 1924, culminating in the hiring of Brookline, Massachusetts, landscape design firm the Olmsted Brothers in 1930. The plan envisioned a long axis ending with the president's home, Flowerhill, plus a new quadrangle of educational buildings. While their plan was not completely followed, much of the campus's redbrick charm remains, even in newer structures. In 1956, the school became coeducational. Rapid expansion of higher education nationwide was witnessed in microcosm locally as the school rapidly grew in enrollment as it became the University of Montevallo with four separate colleges in 1969.

In the past 10 years, the University of Montevallo has expanded its footprint with a classroom building on Main Street and the acquisition and renovation of homes that border on campus. This has increased both student sidewalk foot traffic and town-and-gown interactions. The 2020 completion of the Alan and Lindsey Song Center for the Arts, two blocks from Main Street, has also heightened this phenomenon. The university long operated a golf course, but this is undergoing a transformation to become a pre-eminent mountain biking course that is likely to become a regional attraction.

No one from 1817 would recognize today's city and environs, but a resident from 1917 would note today a number of structures such as King House (built in 1823), Reynolds Hall (1851), Saylor House (1858), Main Hall (1897), McKibbon House (1884), Lyman House (1886), Morgan-Winslett Home (1886), Czeskleba TV (around 1896), Peterson Home (1900), and the First United Methodist Church (1907) that still exist, many of which have been remodeled or updated. Some older campus buildings have not survived into the current century such as Jeter Hall (1915), McCall Pool (1951), or Fuller Hall (1961). While many might miss those buildings and the memories therein, the continued substantial maintenance of these assets outstripped their functionality.

Like nearly all cities in the United States, Montevallo has an annual calendar of regular events that promote civic participation, entertainment, cultural enrichment, and fellowship. Select events include Martin Luther King Jr. Unity March (January), College Night/Homecoming at the University of Montevallo (February), the Annual Festival of Tulips at the American Village (Spring), Montevallo Arts Fest (April), commencement at the University of Montevallo (May and December), Montevallo Farmers' Market (Summer), Independence Day Celebration at the American Village (July), Tinglewood Festival/Cars by the Creek (September), Fire Prevention Day (October), Founders' Day at the University of Montevallo (October), Montevallo Art Walk (October), Veterans Day Observances at the American Village and the Alabama National Cemetery (November), and the Annual Christmas Parade (December). The university has endowed lecture events (Dancy Lectures, Hallie Farmer Lectures, and Fallin Lectures) that bring in prominent speakers. Many of these town-and-gown events date to well over 100 years ago, while others have been added in this current century and are all part of the "past and present" dichotomy.

A reading of Montevallo's past and present affords a longitudinal look at an important Alabama town and its institution of higher education. While many physical buildings and residents may have disappeared, the photographic and archival memories indicate a rich legacy of development, education, recreation, employment, family history, and spiritual enhancement. All human institutions and artifacts undergo periods of renovation and renewal, and Montevallo, both town and university, is fortunate to have retained much of its older charm during various waves of redevelopment.

CHAPTER 1

Academic and Administrative

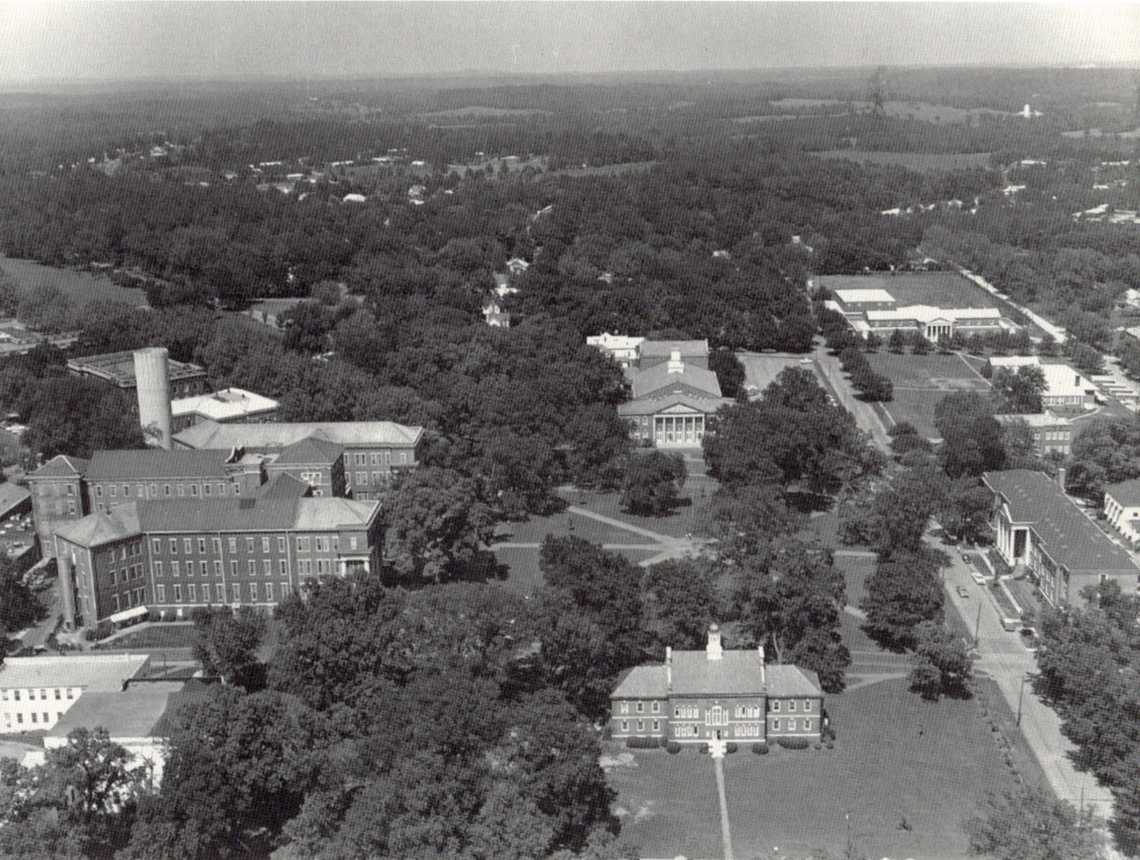

The decade of the 1960s saw Alabama College during its greatest transformation. Enrollment doubled; the school added four academic buildings, a library, and a student union; and it became the University of Montevallo. This c. 1965 photograph shows the core of the main campus, with Main Hall Dormitory (left) and Calkins and Palmer Halls facing each other across the Main Quad.

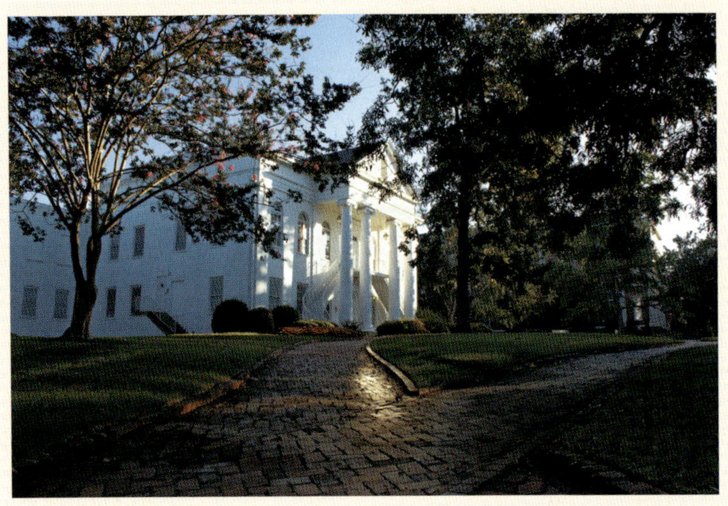

The neoclassical Reynolds Hall, built in 1851, is the oldest academic building on campus and served many functions in its early years including chapel, gymnasium, post office, space for classrooms, and supply store. Alabama College named the building in 1925 after the first university president, Henry Clay Reynolds, who was a local merchant and newspaper publisher. This c. 1897 photograph shows Reynolds Hall in the foreground and the first constructed wing of Main Hall, Elizabeth Haley, on the right.

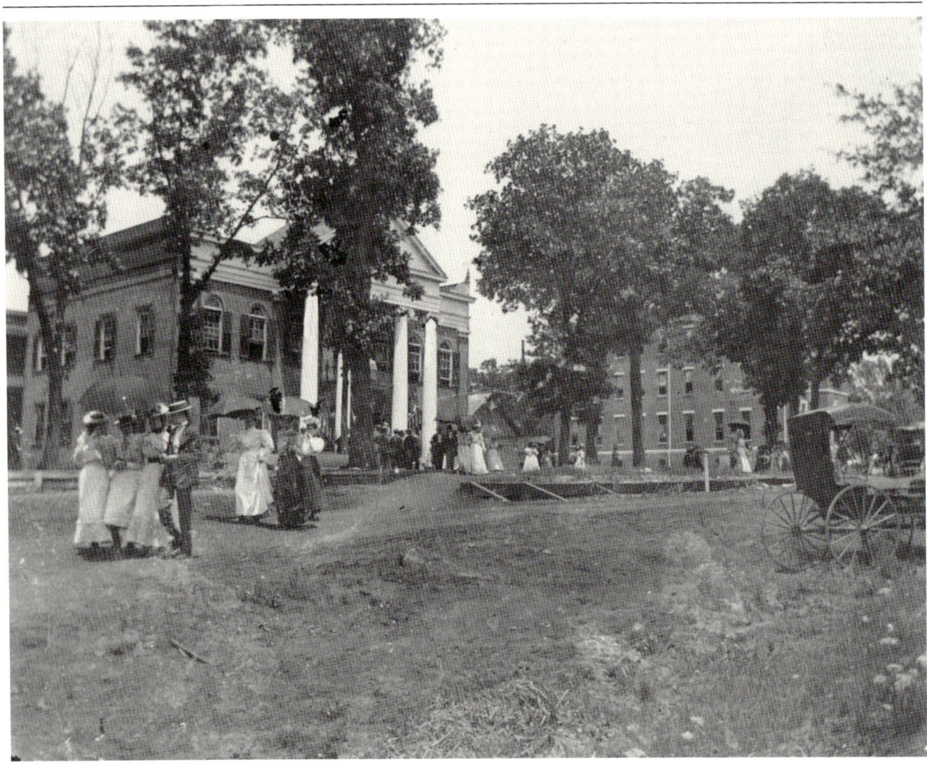

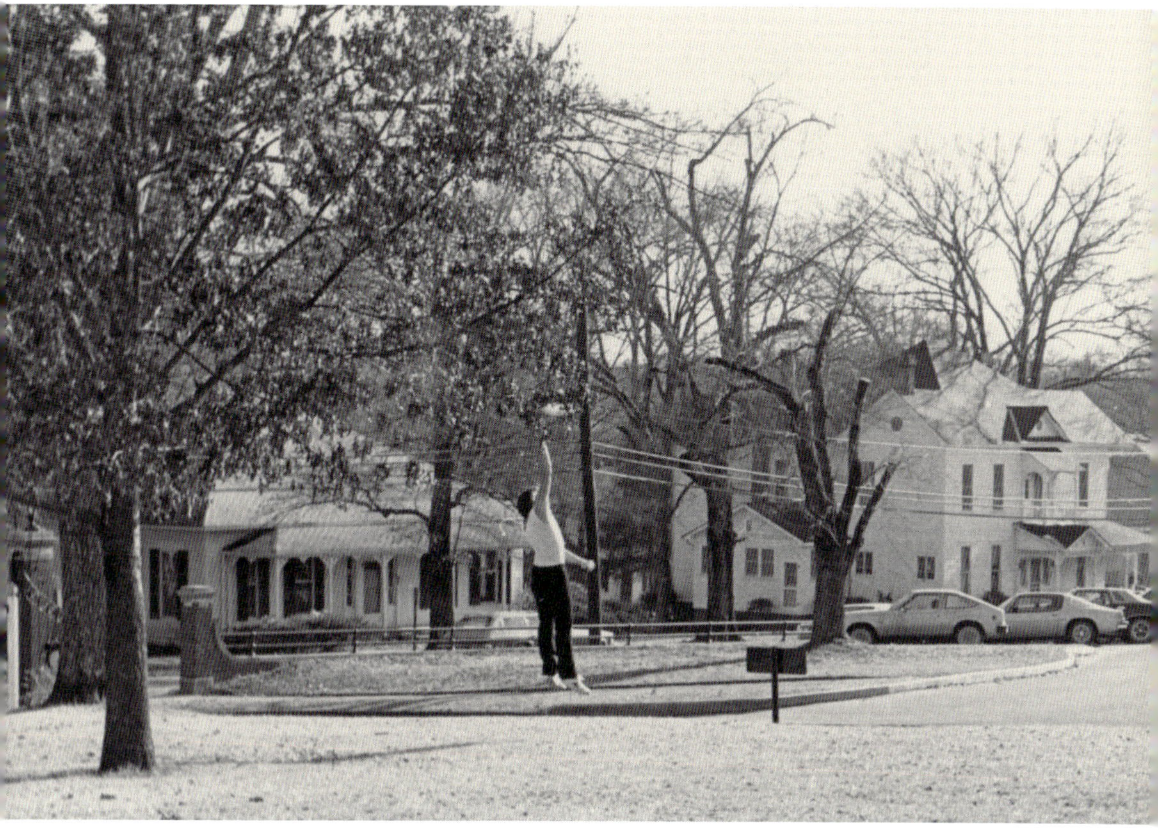

Will Lyman was a civic leader and banking official and served as mayor from 1916 to 1918. The Lyman family built two adjoining houses in the mid- to late 1800s, a one-story structure with Greek Revival trim later named the Van Tuyll House (left) and an Eastlake-style Victorian home (right), the Will Lyman House. The university uses both homes as offices, including human resources and the Falcon Success Center. Hendrik Van Tuyll was a beloved longtime professor of philosophy.

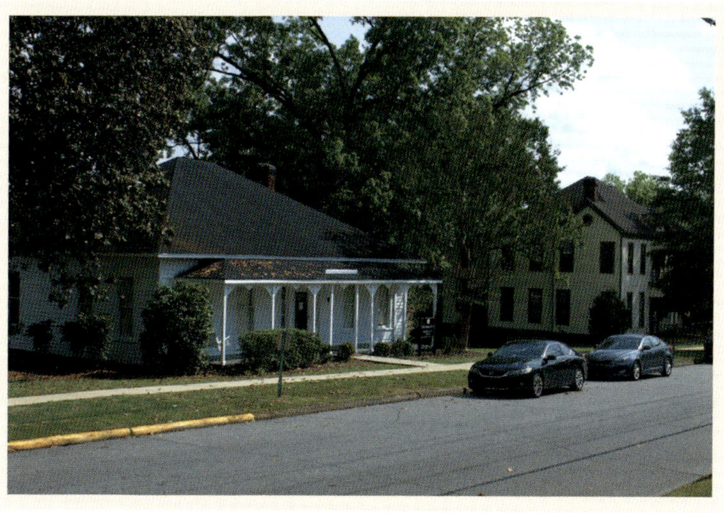

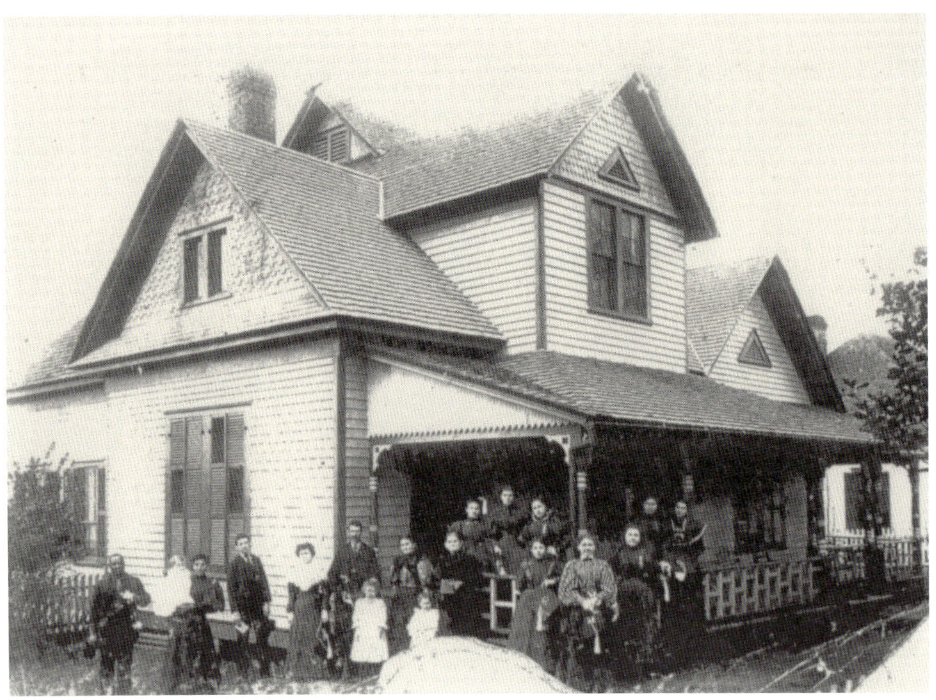

Built in 1886 by local businessperson C.L. (Charles Lloyd) Meroney, Meroney House represents the Eastlake style. Meroney and his wife, Ellen, raised four daughters in the home, including Eloise, a long-serving English professor who lived in the house until her death in 1996. Sensing a chance for local economic growth, he actively helped to recruit the Alabama Girls' Industrial School to Montevallo and served as an original board of trustees member.

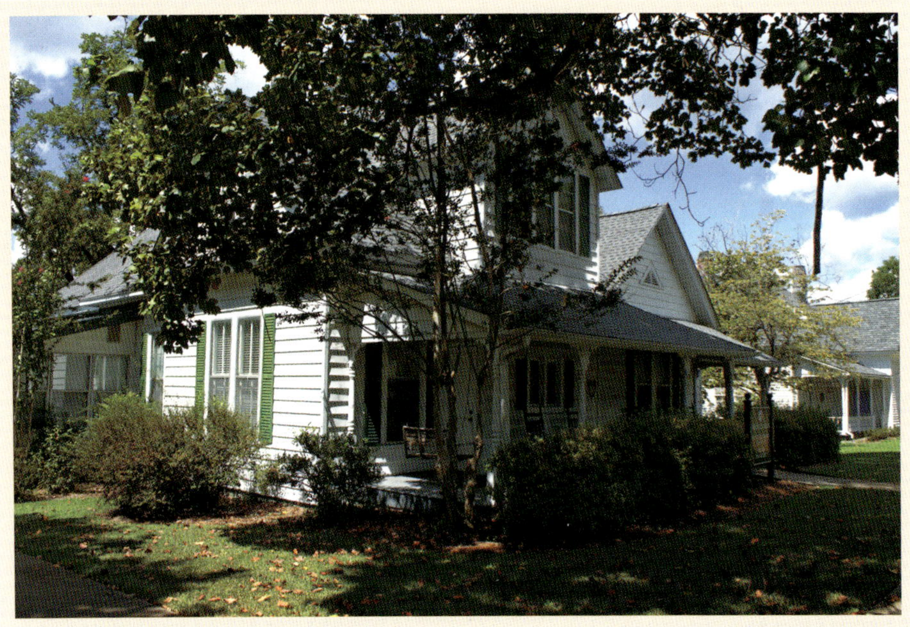

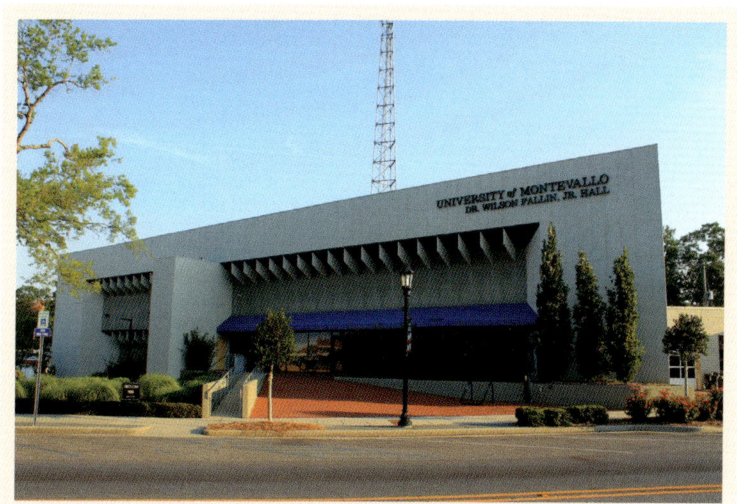

The Owl's Cove was a Victorian-era home built by Austrian-born George Kroell around 1900. The home was demolished in the early 1960s. In 1975, Alabama Power built the current structure to house its local office. In 2013, the city, county, and university remodeled it to accommodate the Department of Behavioral and Social Sciences, and the university named it in honor of Dr. Wilson Fallin Jr. in 2022. Fallin Hall's micropark is named Owl's Cove Park to recognize the previous structure.

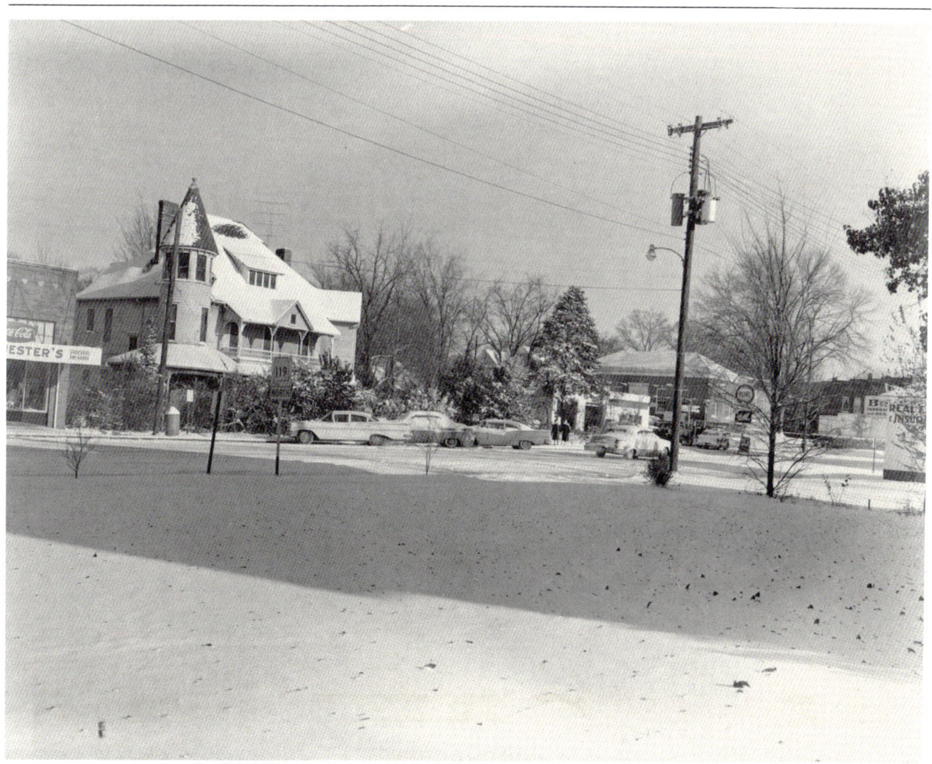

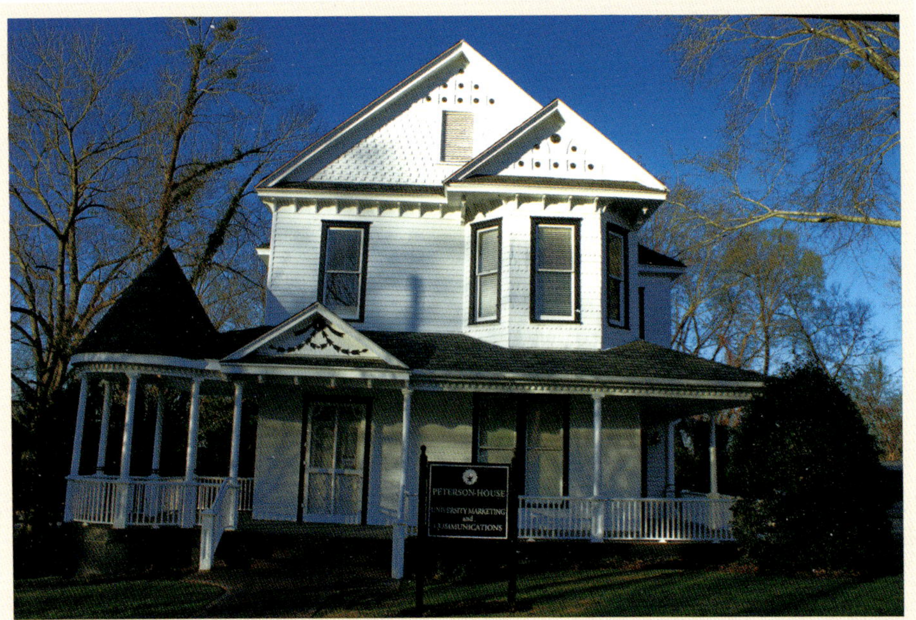

Francis Marion Peterson was the second president of the school from 1899 to 1907. Originally a Hebrew scholar, classicist, and minister, he became an academic administrator in the 1880s. Peterson navigated the school through difficult financial times.

Peterson House, built after 1900 by Lucy Cary, is an Eastlake-style Victorian home. The city's first radio set aired the results of the 1916 presidential election here. The university renovated the home in 2013, and it now houses University Marketing and Communications.

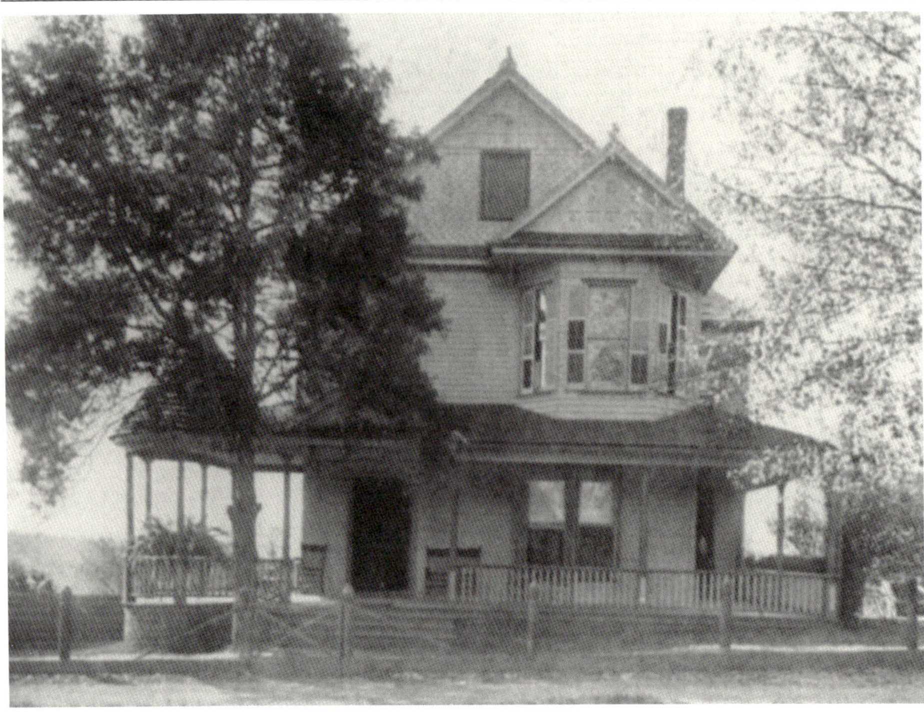

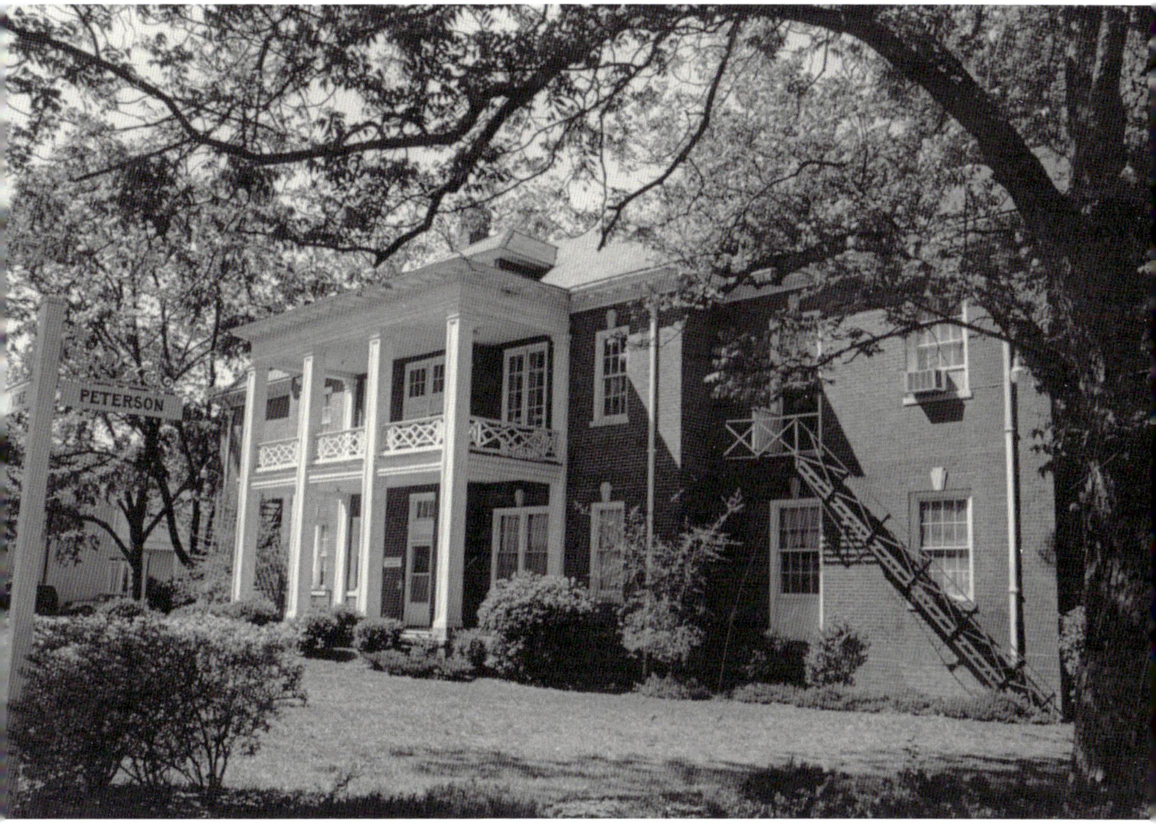

King House acted as an infirmary when first purchased by the school in the summer of 1908. Peterson Hall, seen here, completed in 1914, served as the medical facility for six decades. Student Condie Cunningham's fatal accident (1908) in Main Hall, as well as several rounds of communicable diseases, caused the board of trustees to task Pres. Thomas Palmer with securing professional health care. He hired Dr. Willena Peck from Boston, Massachusetts, to act as the first on-campus physician.

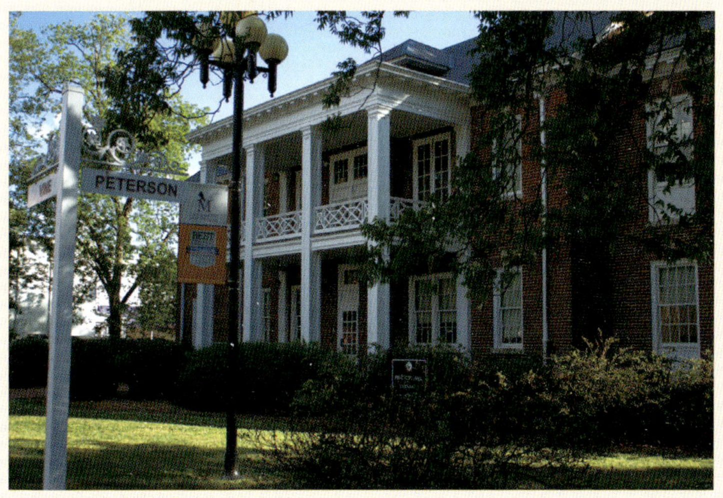

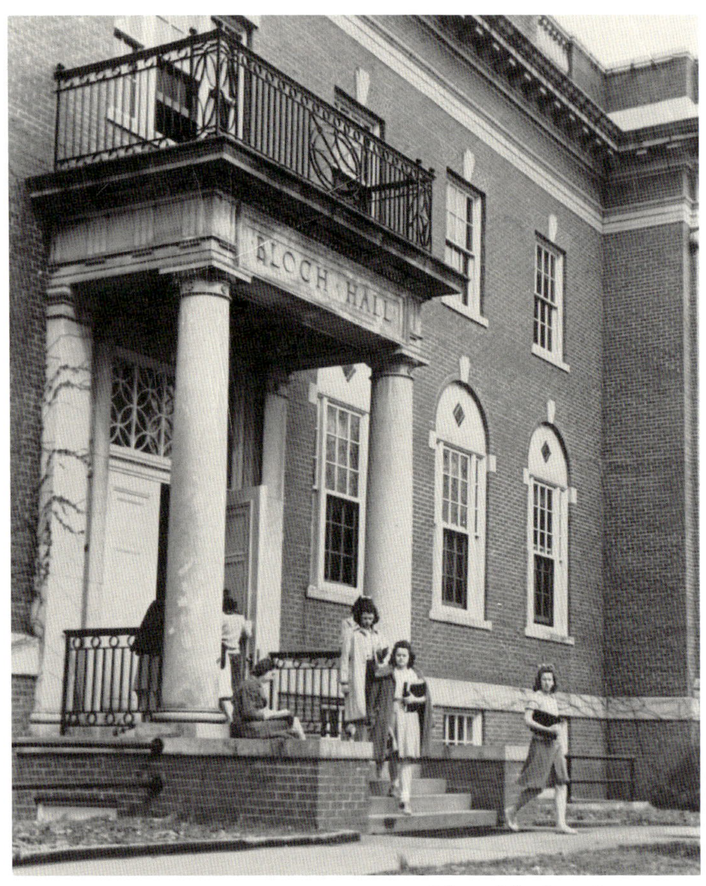

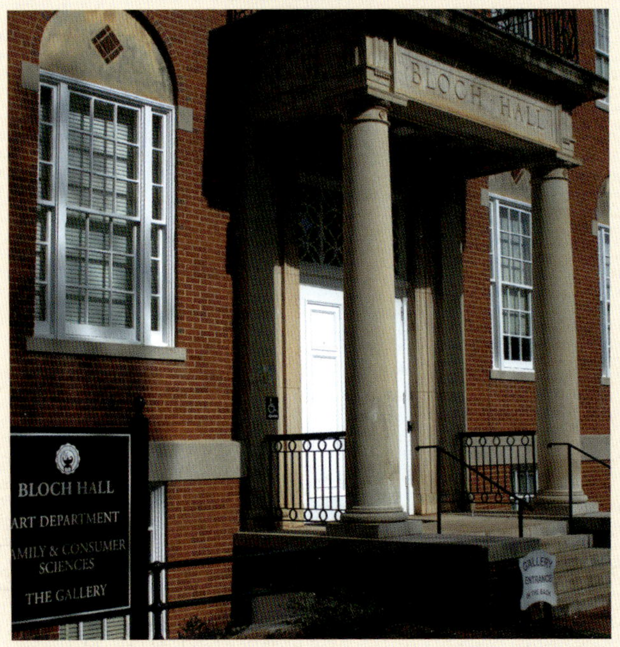

Named for longtime Alabama legislator Solomon Bloch, Bloch Hall provided a state-of-the-art classroom experience after its construction. The building featured running water, electricity, and gas and provided a laboratory space for science as well as cooking classes. Completed in 1915, the building was the first to serve a purely academic mission. Today, the building is home to the art department, Bloch Art Gallery, and the Family and Consumer Sciences program.

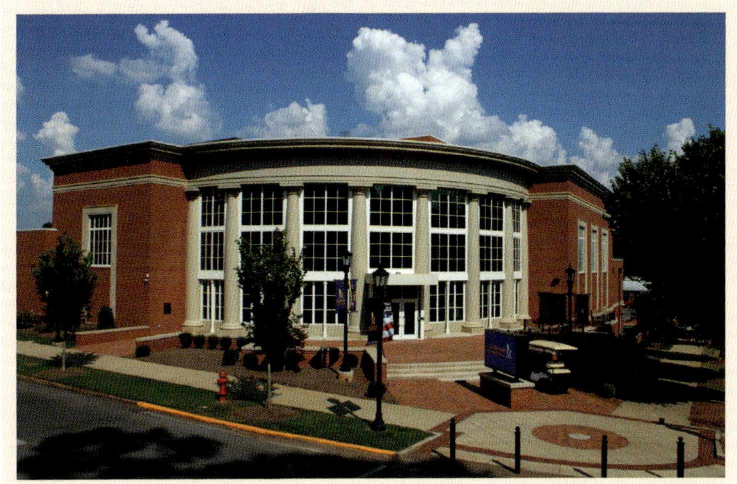

Constructed in 1915 as an elementary school, Jeter Hall served the city for nearly 50 years. The university bought and renovated it to house the Department of Behavioral and Social Sciences from 1965 to 2013. The university razed the building and in 2020 completed the Alan and Lindsey Song Center for the Arts. This state-of-the-art building houses two performance venues, an art gallery, classrooms, theater faculty, vocal performance rehearsal rooms, and a dance studio.

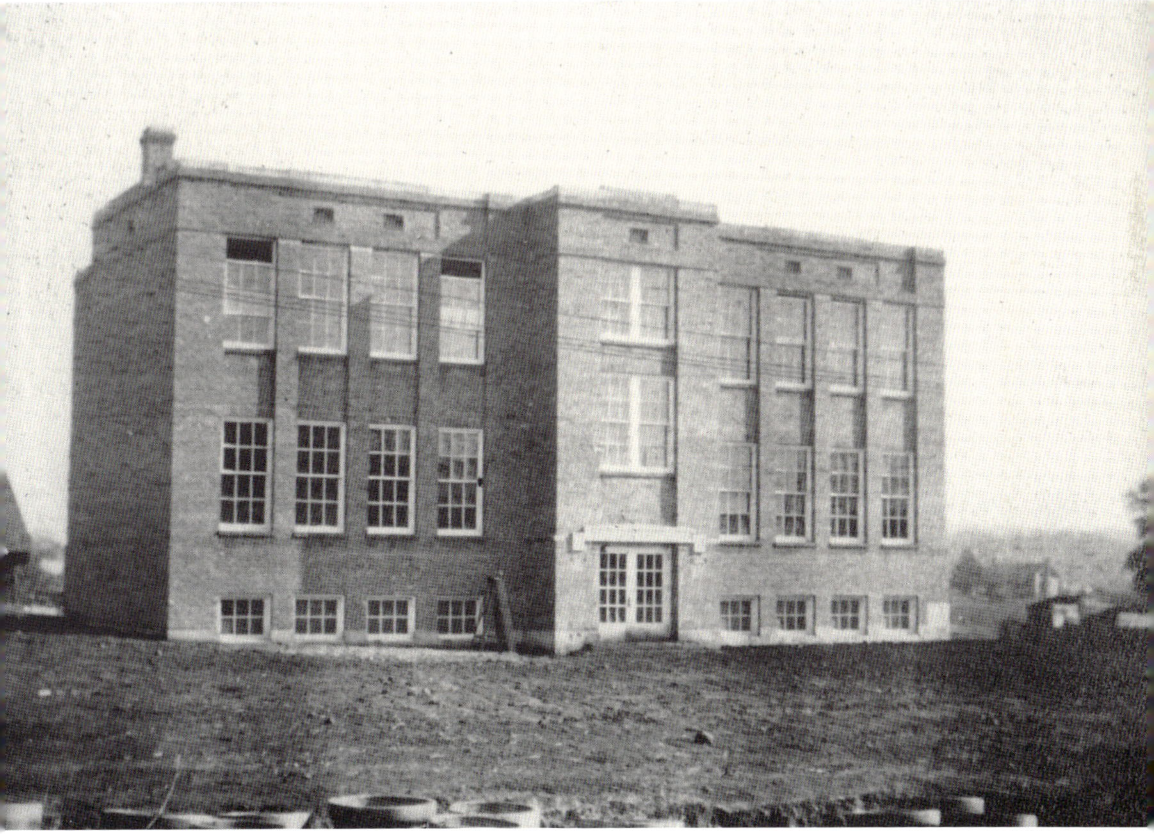

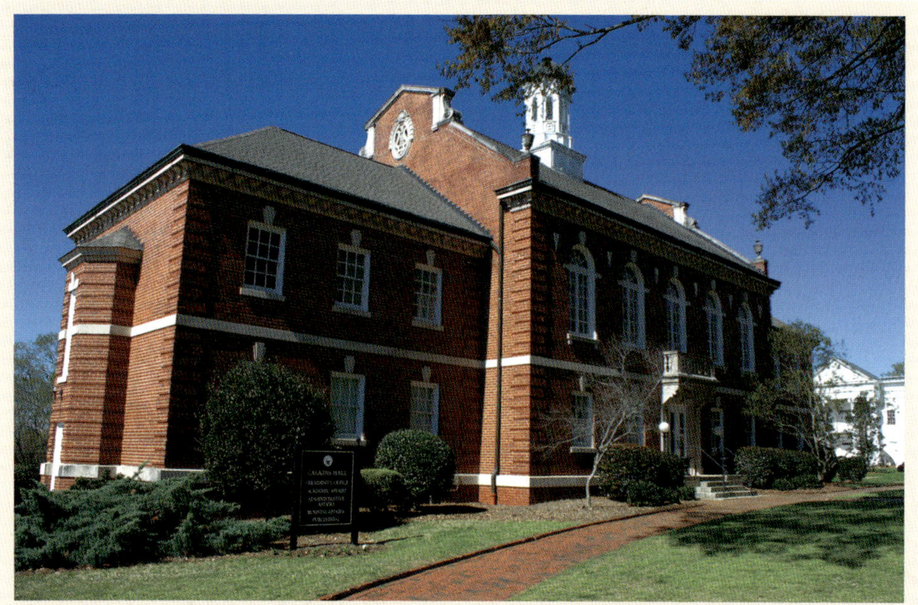

Alabama Girls' Technical Institute completed Calkins Hall, a Colonial Williamsburg–style structure, in 1917 to serve its expanding music program, chaired by Prof. Charles Calkins. Soon after his death in 1921, the school named the building in his memory. In 1973, the university renovated and repurposed Calkins as its administrative building, housing the president's and provost's offices, as well as the original board of trustees' boardroom and various business offices.

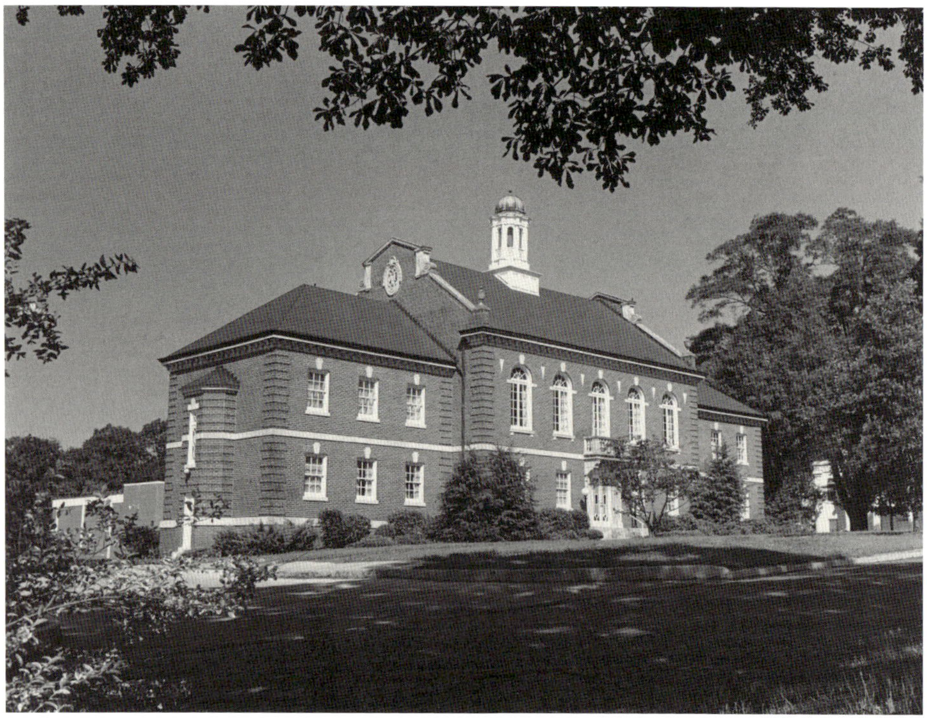

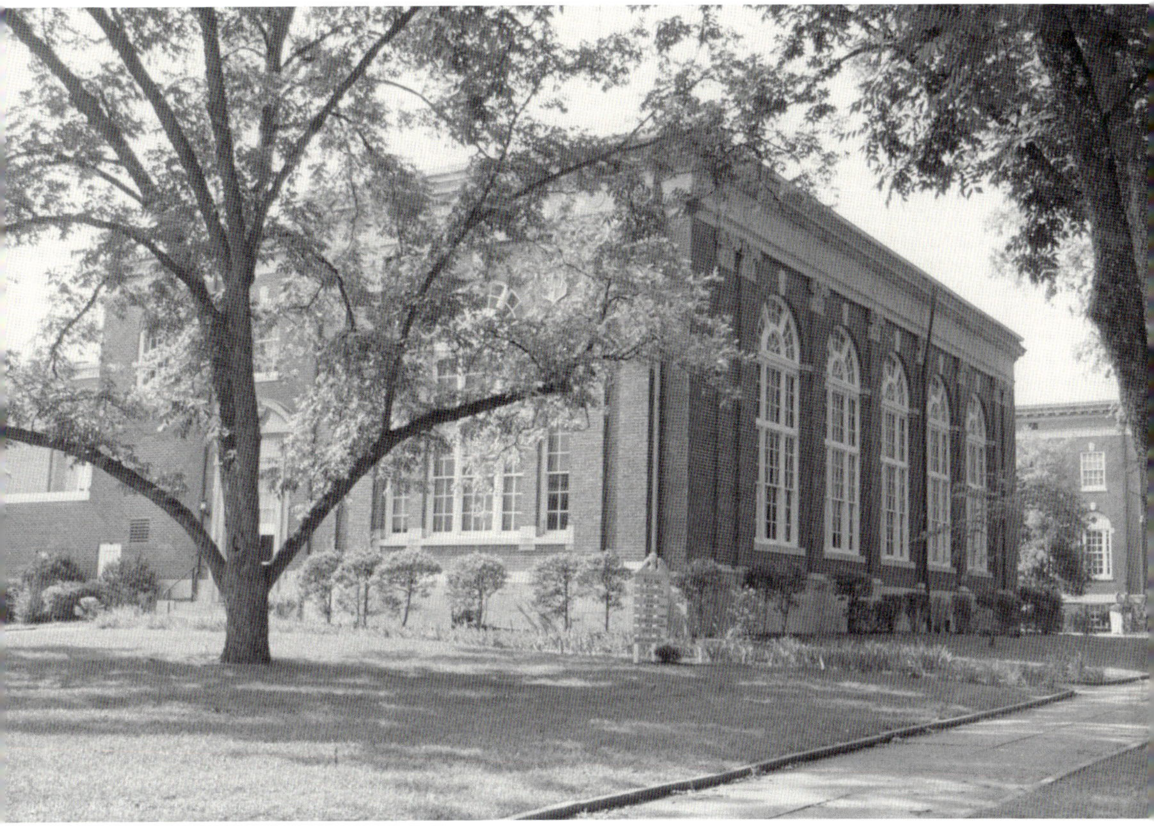

After the school's founding in 1896, its library was in several locations. In 1923, the newly named Alabama College completed its first standalone library, Wills Hall, which featured a 90-foot reading room with Palladian windows. By the 1960s, the university built a new library, and a renovated and enlarged Wills housed the College of Education and Human Development. Edward Wills served the school in several roles, notably registrar and business manager, from 1909 to 1946.

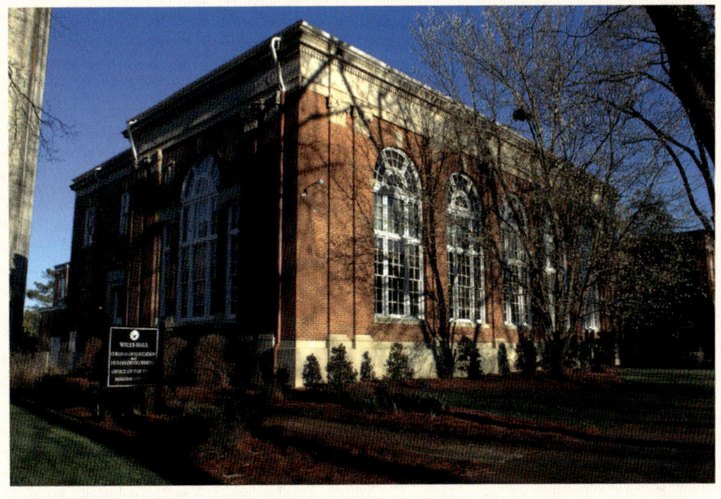

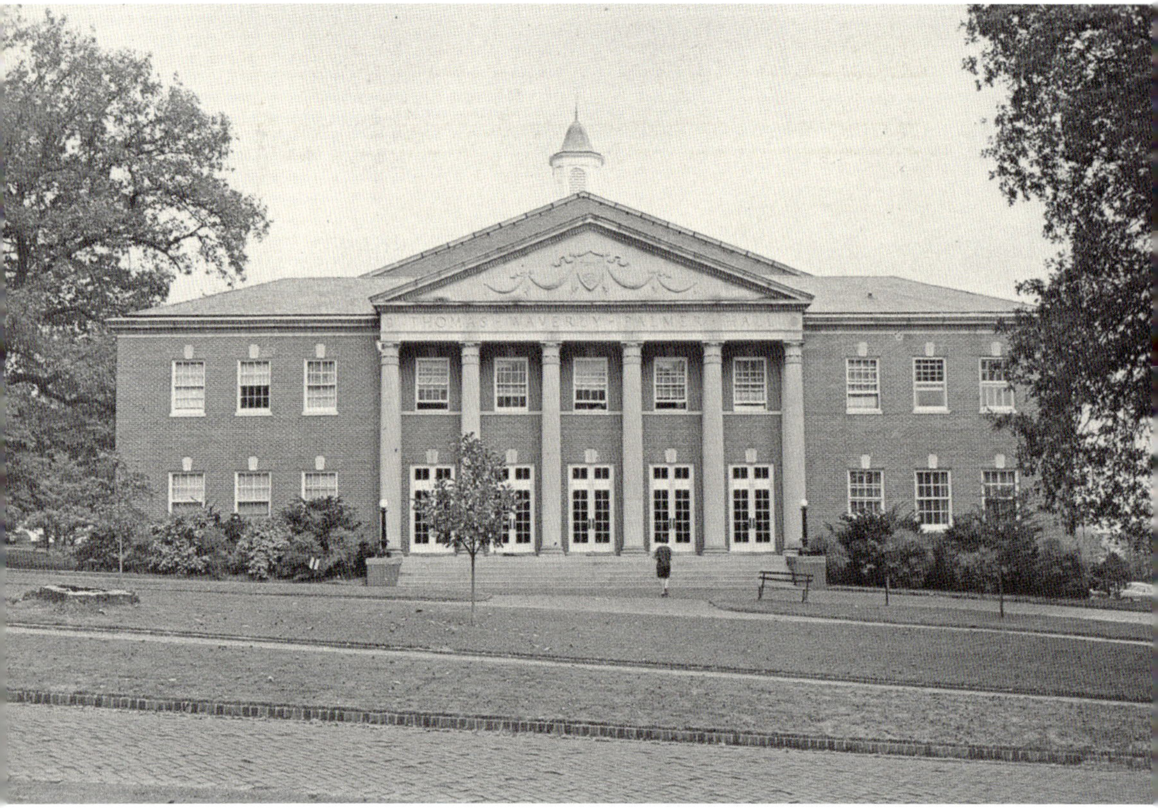

Built in 1929, Palmer Hall provided much-needed theater, convocation, concert, and lecture space. The Alabama College administration, business manager, and registrar offices also occupied the building. The 1,200-seat interior is based on the Volksbühne in Berlin, Germany. Named for Pres. Thomas Palmer, who died just a few years earlier, the building is still home to the registrar's office and hosts Founders' Day and College Night, the university's homecoming tradition, since 1930.

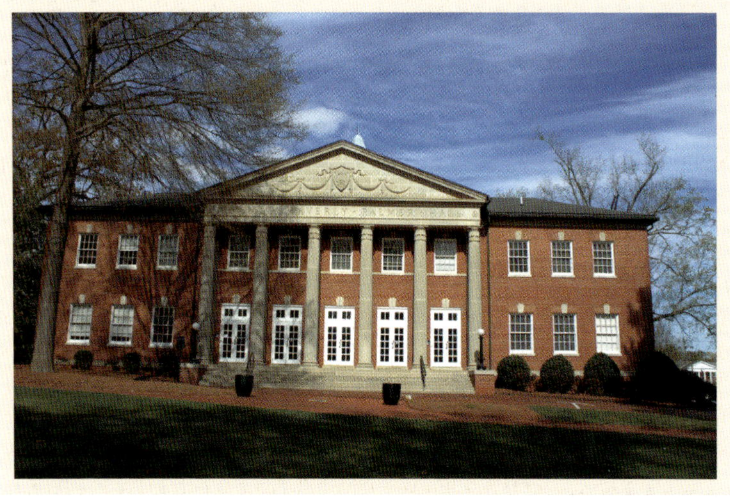

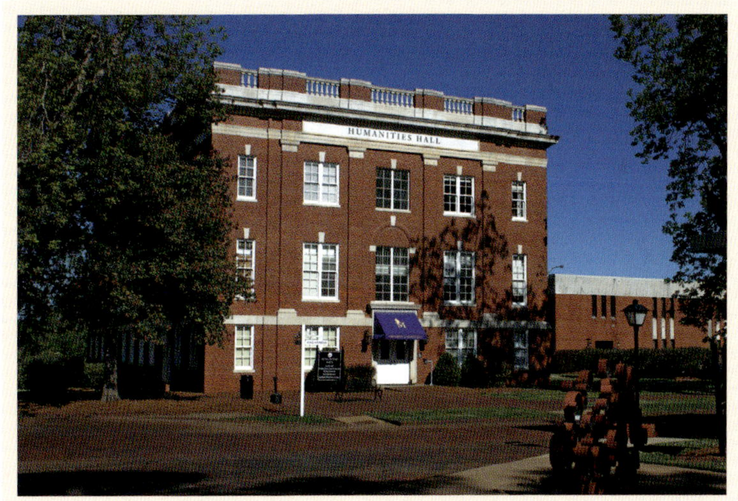

Built in 1940 with funding from the Works Progress Administration and originally named after Alabama governor Braxton Bragg Comer, this building served as the core home of most academic programs for Alabama College well into the late 1950s. It also was the site for the campus radio station, WAPI. Today, named Humanities Hall, it houses the Department of English and World Languages, an auditorium, the Sarah G. Palmer Commons room, and the Harbert Writing Center.

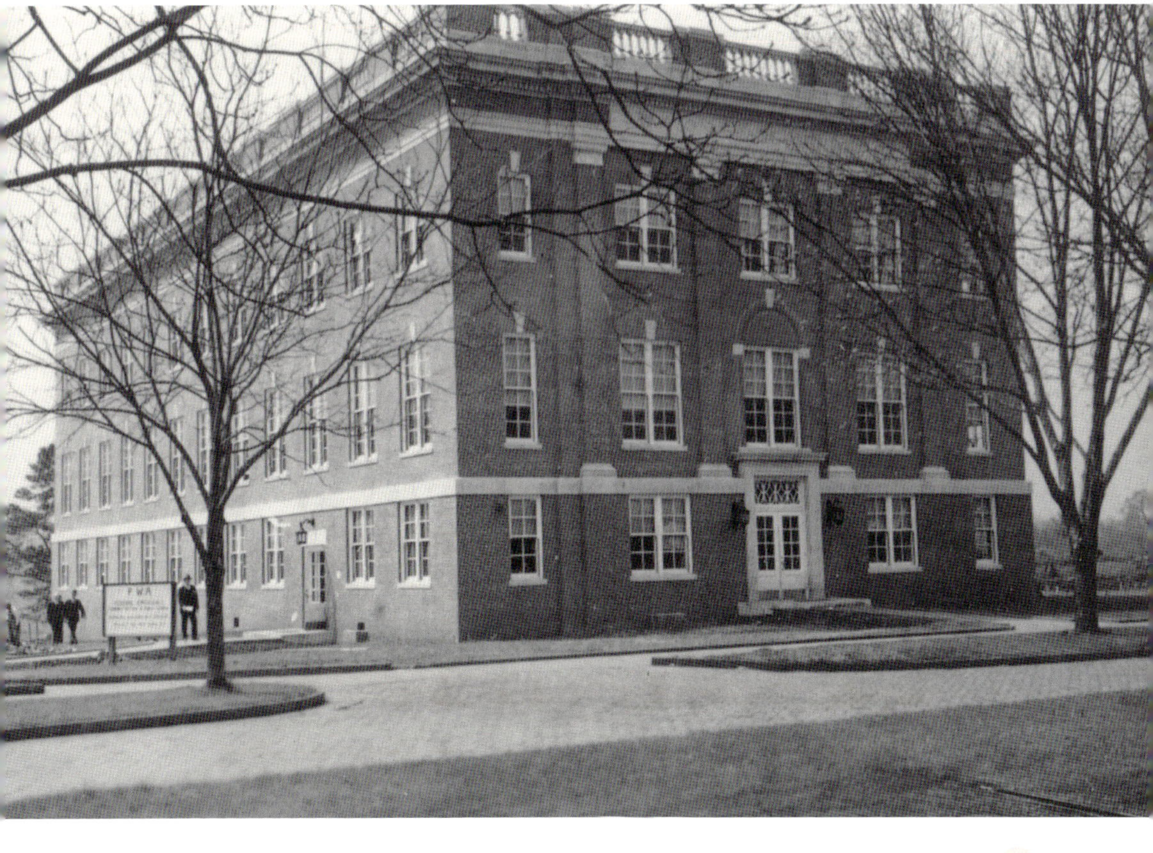

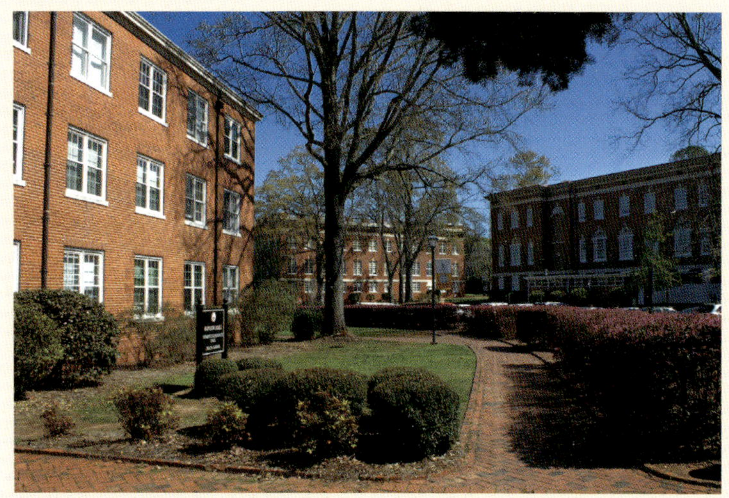

These images feature Hanson Hall (left), Humanities Hall (center), and Bloch Hall (right). The women's dormitory (Hanson) and the two classroom buildings highlight the campus's use of bricks. The natural attributes of central Alabama allow for easy brick manufacturing. By 1930, Alabama College administrators had enlisted the services of the Olmsted Brothers Architectural Firm to design a landscape and building plan for the school. Construction of all buildings, streets, and sidewalks adheres to this near-century-old plan.

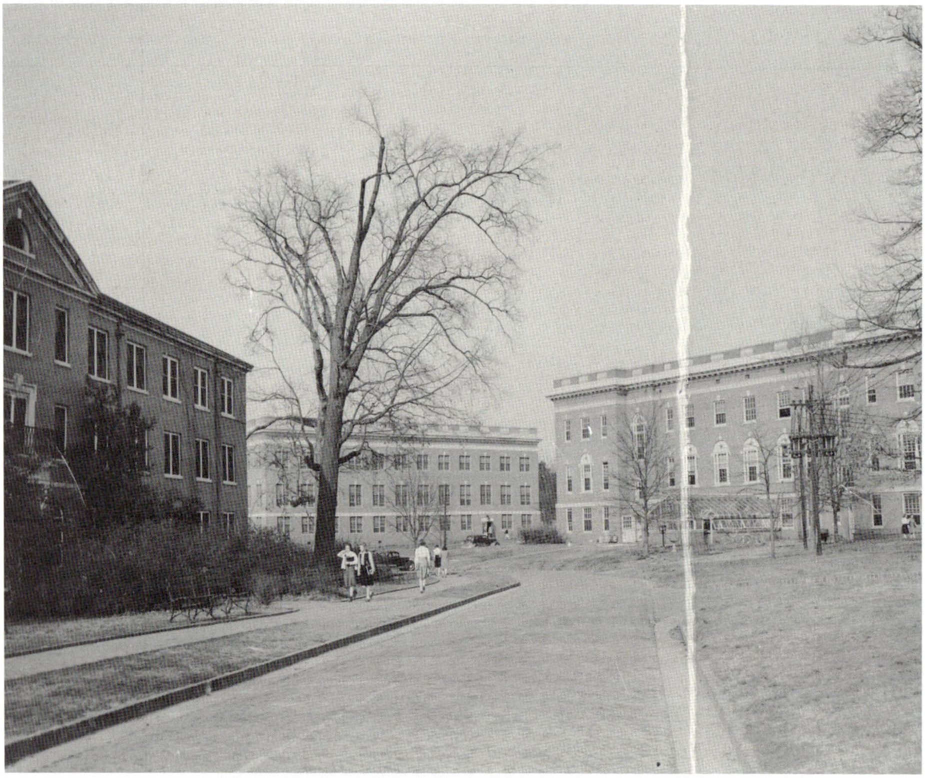

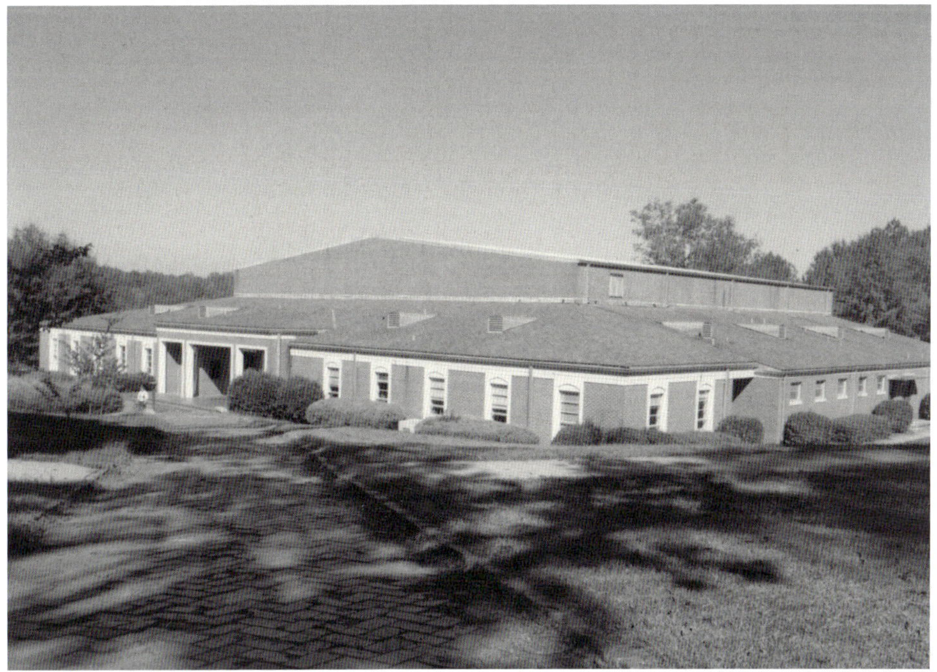

By the early 1960s, Alabama College's athletic facilities no longer met the needs of the growing student body and the addition of officially sanctioned sports teams, including men's basketball. Completed in 1964, Myrick Hall offered a 30,000-square-foot complex with physical education classrooms, faculty offices, locker rooms, and a 2,000-seat basketball court. In 1967, the school named it for alumna and physical education professor Geneva Myrick, who had passed away unexpectedly. Myrick Hall will house Montevallo's new nursing program.

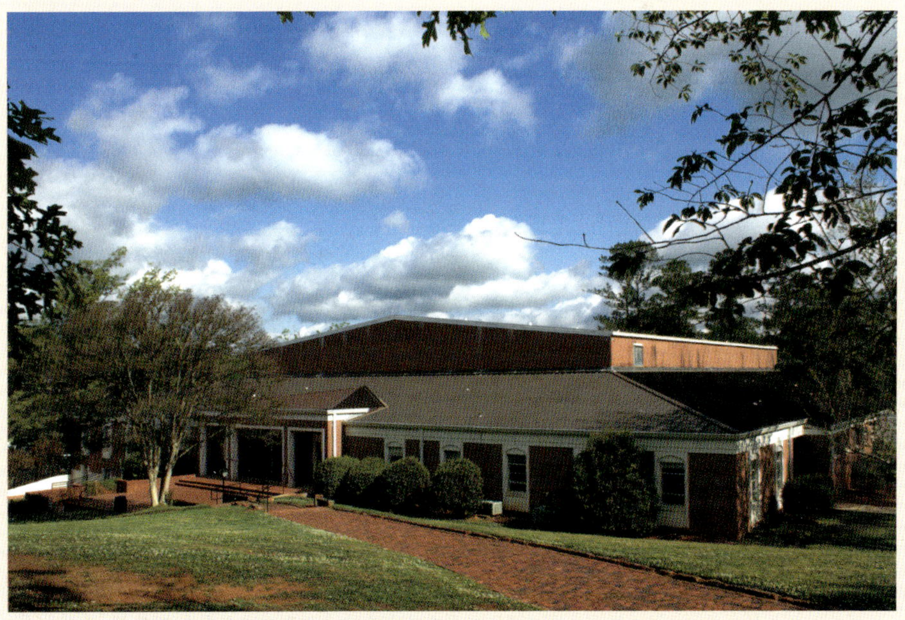

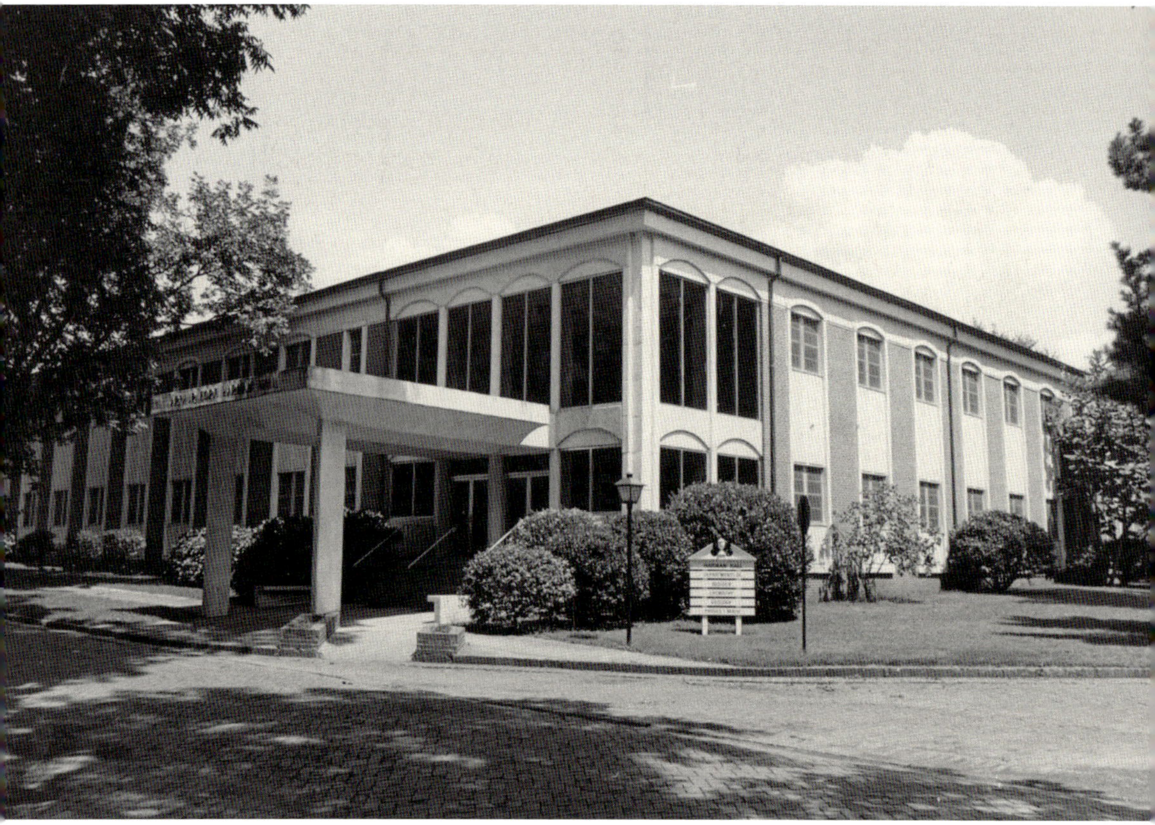

Arthur Fort Harman served as Alabama College president from 1935 to 1947, shepherding the institution during the Great Depression and war. With a rapidly expanding student body, the school constructed a new science building, Harman Hall, in 1968. It features a central courtyard with an eight-ton geode and a memorial to World War II veteran and biology professor Eugene B. Sledge. Sledge's memoir, *With the Old Breed*, is one of the finest works of war literature.

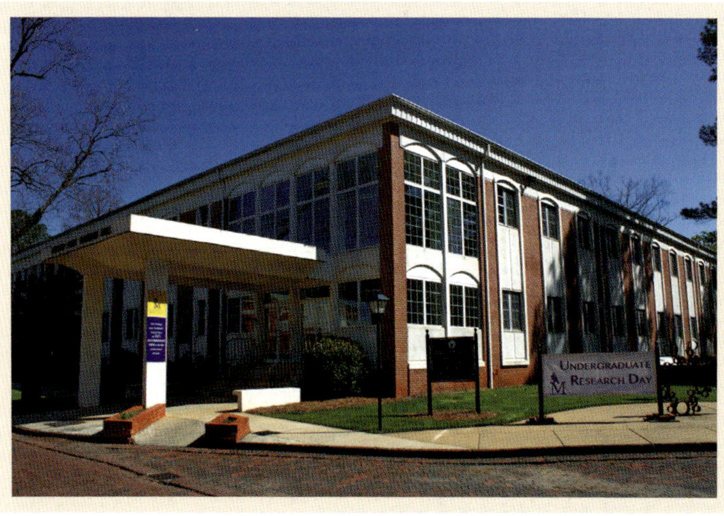

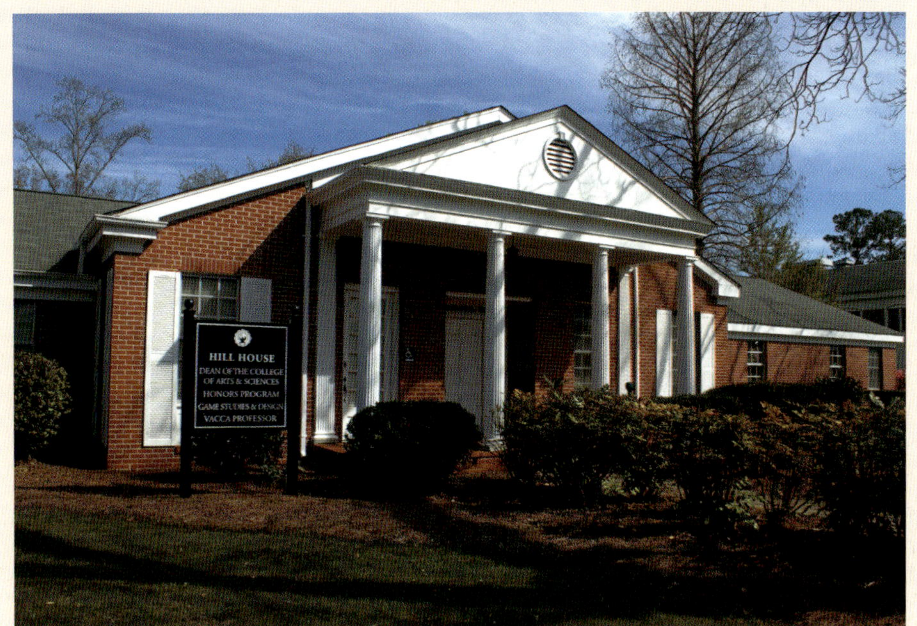

Elizabeth Baldwin Hill was a three-term member of the Alabama College Board of Trustees. Upon her death in 1961, a faculty resolution named her "one of the ablest trustees and one of its most enthusiastic friends." Hill Hall, completed in 1967, originally served as the Home Economics Laboratory, including an apartment for the director. Long the home of the dean of the College of Arts & Sciences, it now houses the Malone Center for Excellence in Teaching.

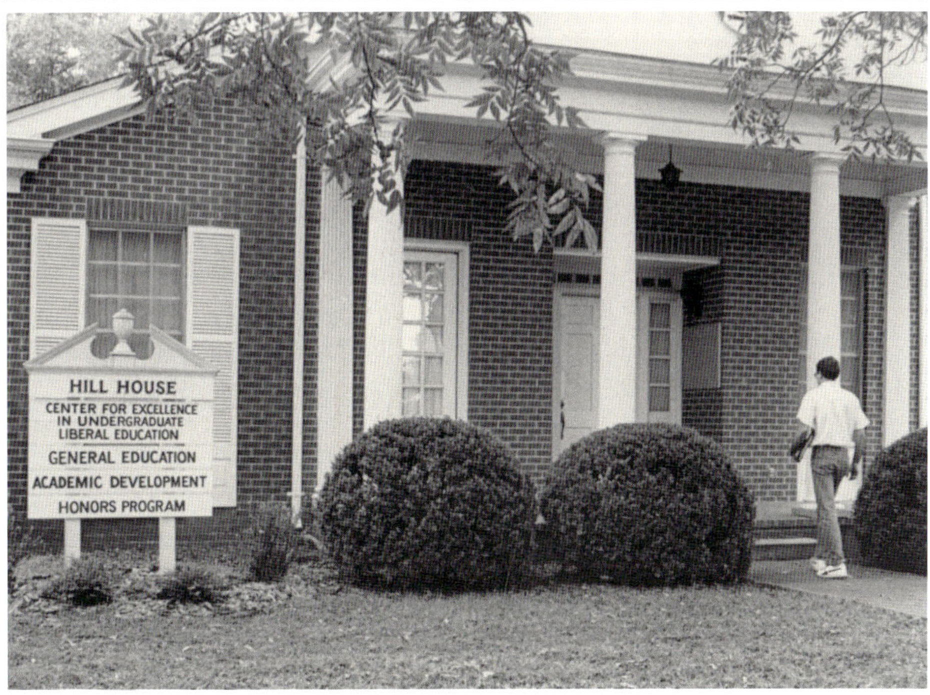

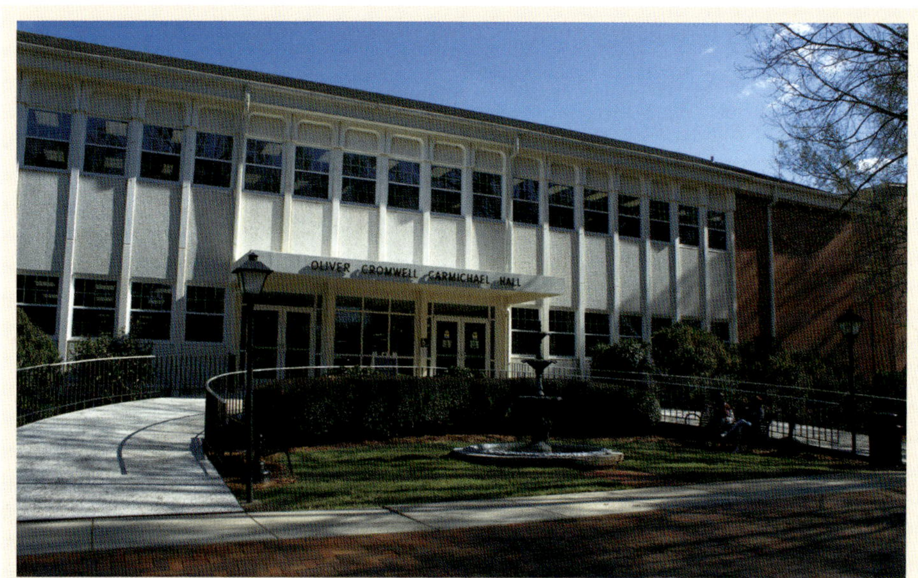

Named for Alabama College president Oliver Cromwell Carmichael, the current library opened in 1968 and features three floors of stacks, meeting spaces, and campus amenities such as the Anna Crawford Milner Archives and Special Collections, the Pat Scales Special Collections Room, the Digital Media Lab, the Learning Enrichment Center, and the Information Services and Technology Helpdesk. As of 2022, Carmichael Hall houses over 185,000 print titles.

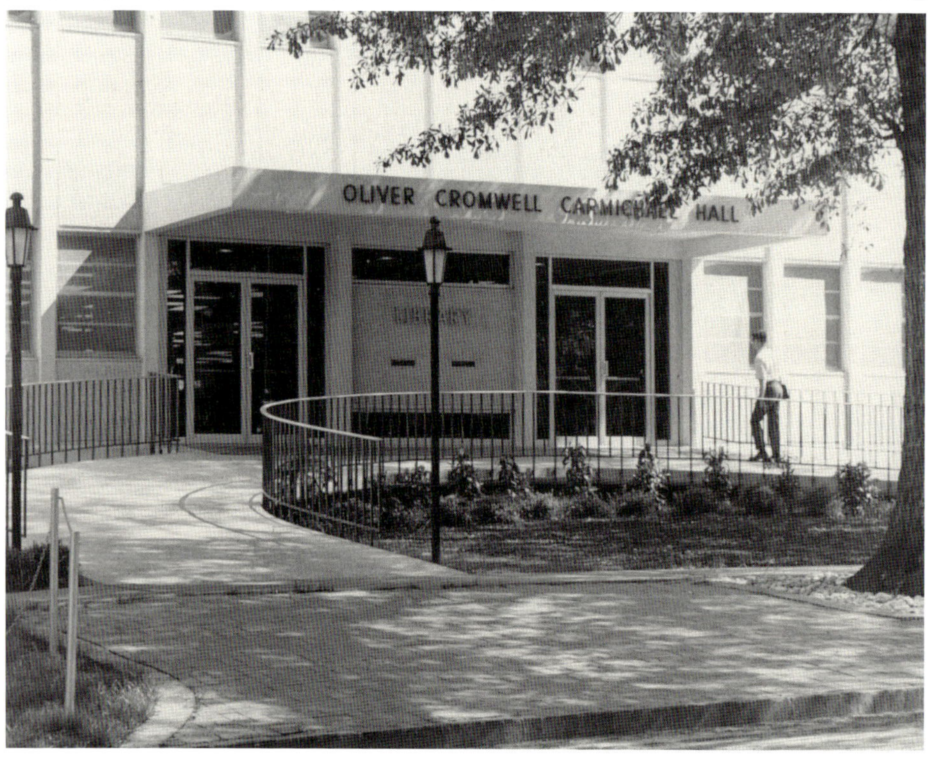

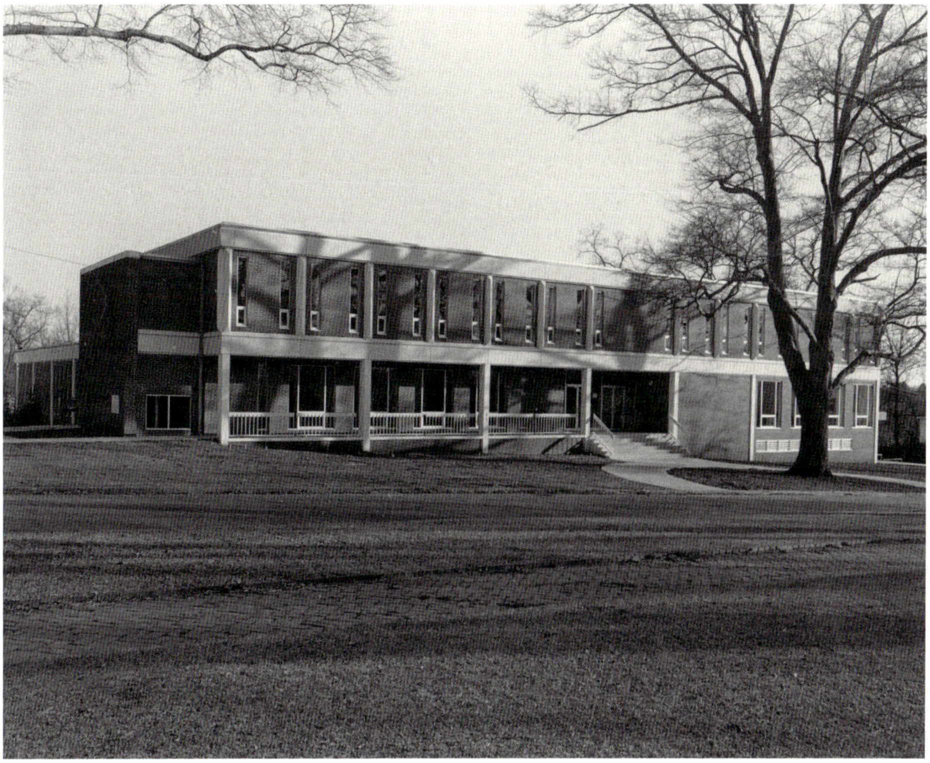

The school's impressive reputation for music education resulted in an expansion of course offerings and the number of faculty and students in the 1960s. To accommodate this growth, the university completed the Dr. Maxine Couch Davis Hall in 1974. The structure features a 250-seat auditorium, LeBaron Recital Hall. The piano program in the Department of Music received an "All-Steinway" designation in 2007. The department hosts the Young Musicians' Camp every summer, which offers a residential experience for 11- to 18-year-olds.

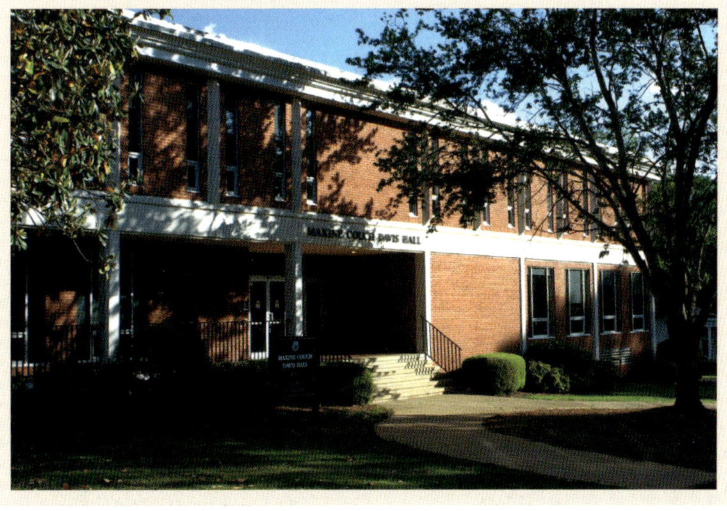

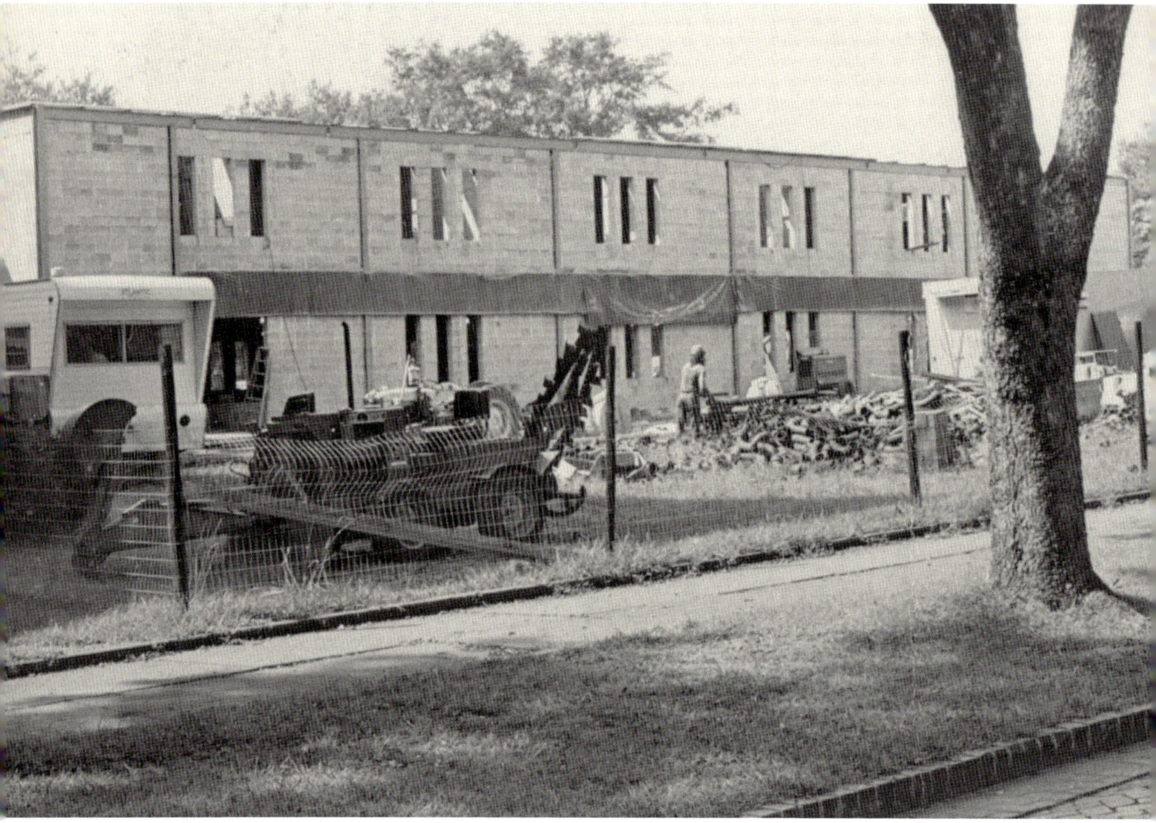

With the creation of the University of Montevallo in 1969, the Department of Business became the College of Business. As its home in Humanities Hall became too crowded with faculty and students, the university completed a new building in 1980 solely for the college named Morgan Hall after longtime business faculty member Sara Posey Morgan. On October 9, 1997, the university officially named the school the Michael E. Stephens College of Business.

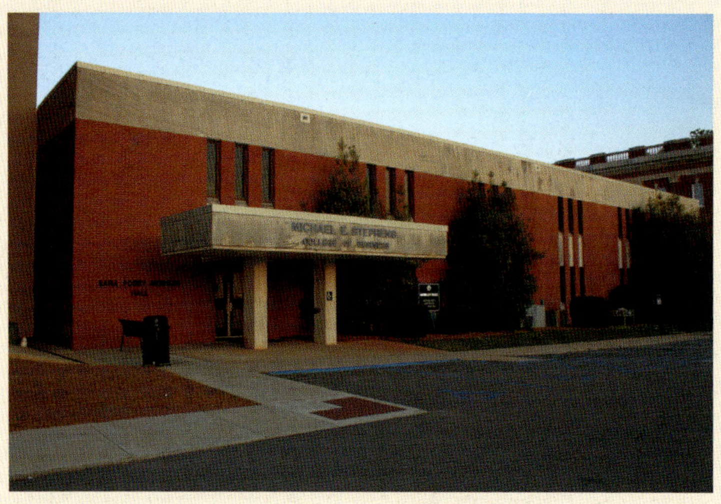

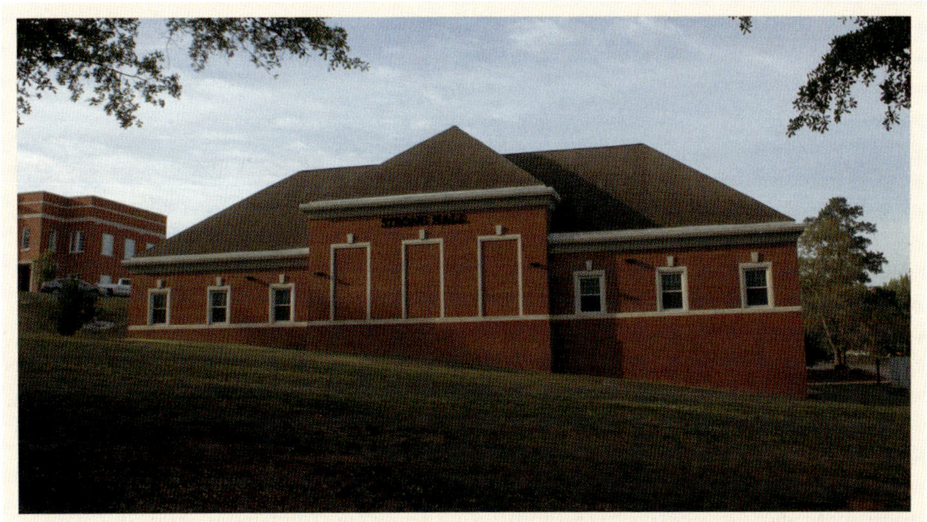

Originally erected as the Mass Communication Building in the 1990s and seen here under construction, the university expanded the structure as Strong Hall in 2017 for the growing Department of Communication with sponsorship from alumni John Paul Strong and his father, Mike Strong. The new addition included faculty offices, classrooms, computer labs, edit bay and video production rooms, a master control room, and a broadcast studio. The department features a weekly student broadcast called *Vallo Vision News.*

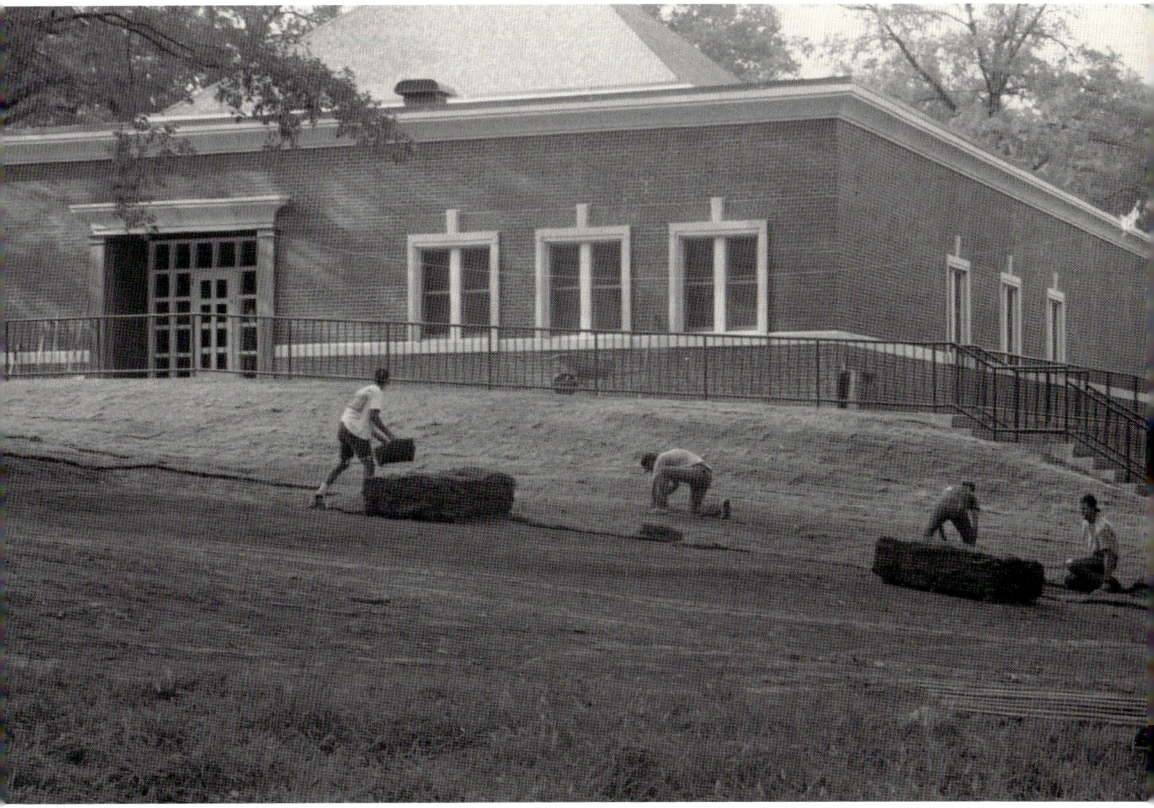

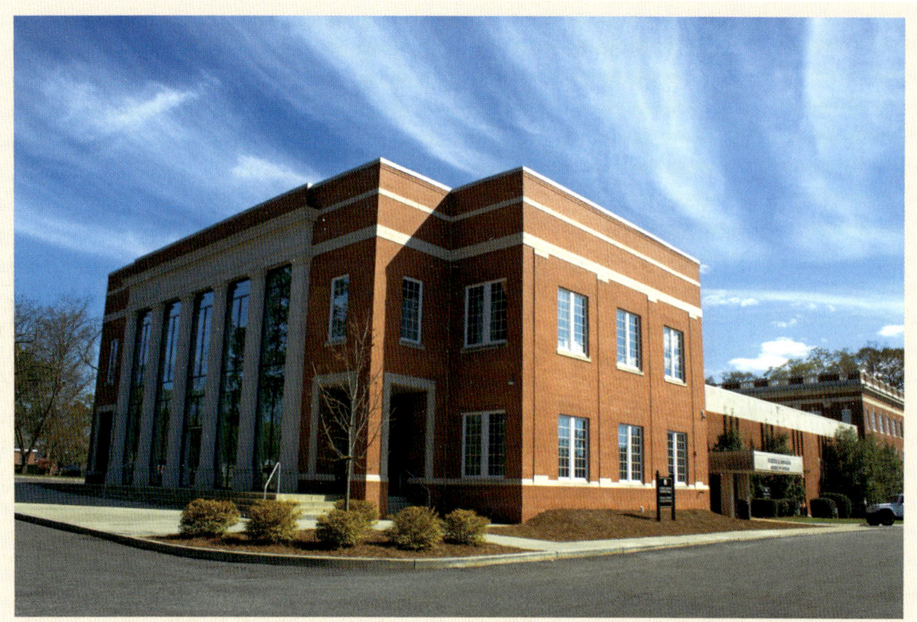

In 2020, the University of Montevallo expanded Morgan Hall with a new addition, Stephens Hall, named after donors Allison and the late Michael E. Stephens. The university opened and dedicated this new facility in 2021. The building includes a student commons, a boardroom, and technology-enhanced classrooms. A 1973 Montevallo alumnus, Michael E. Stephens founded the Lakeshore Foundation in Birmingham to bridge the gaps in services for those needing physical rehabilitation.

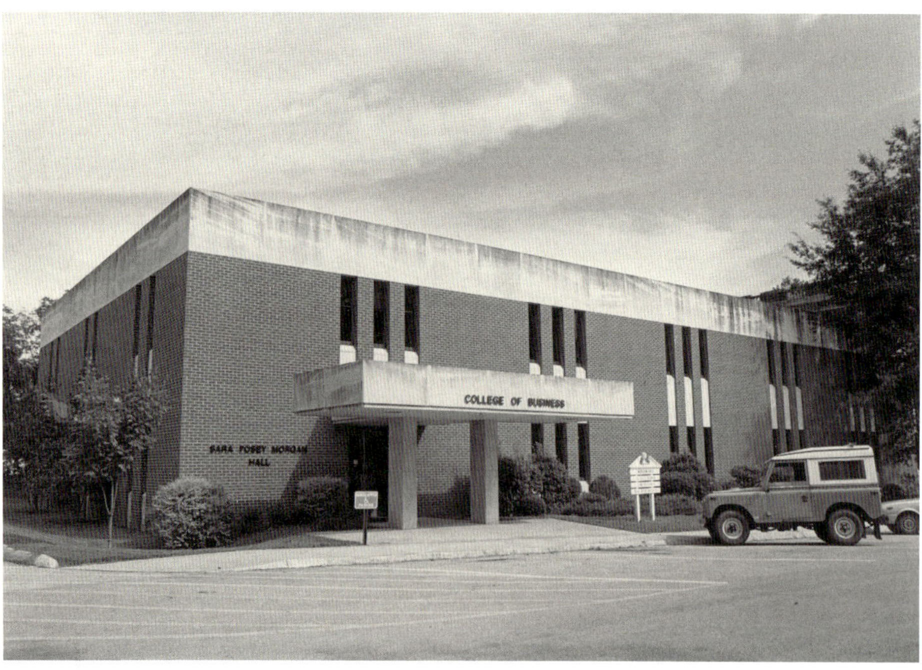

CHAPTER 2

STUDENT LIFE AND CAMPUS FEATURES

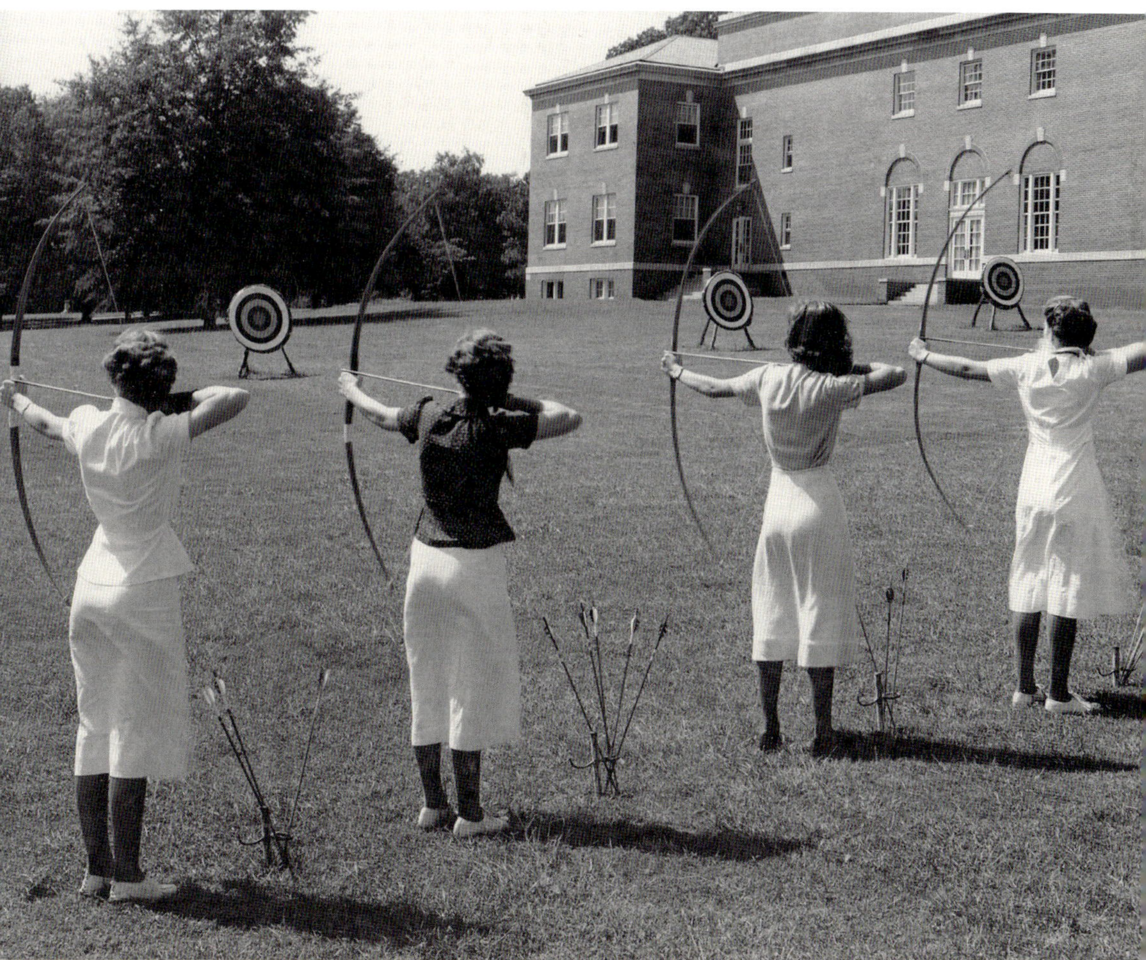

Since the creation of the institution in 1896, students have had multiple campus resources that have supported and enriched their experiences at the school. Be it dormitories, dining halls, or recreational sites, the university, for being a small school, has offered a wide variety of opportunities including a lake, a golf course, a swamp, and a dairy farm.

This image features King House (built in 1823), the first local building constructed with bricks. Reynolds Hall (1851) and Saylor House (1858) were also two early brick structures. During the institution's history, the building has had several functions: infirmary, model house for home economics, dormitory space, office and clinical space for psychology, and currently, a guesthouse for visiting dignitaries. In the 1970s, the university restored King House back to its original Federal-style architectural design.

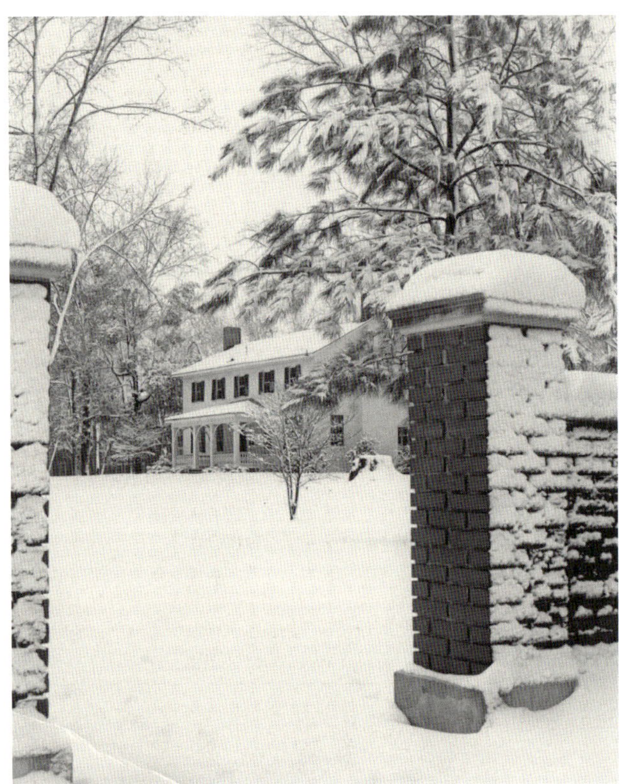

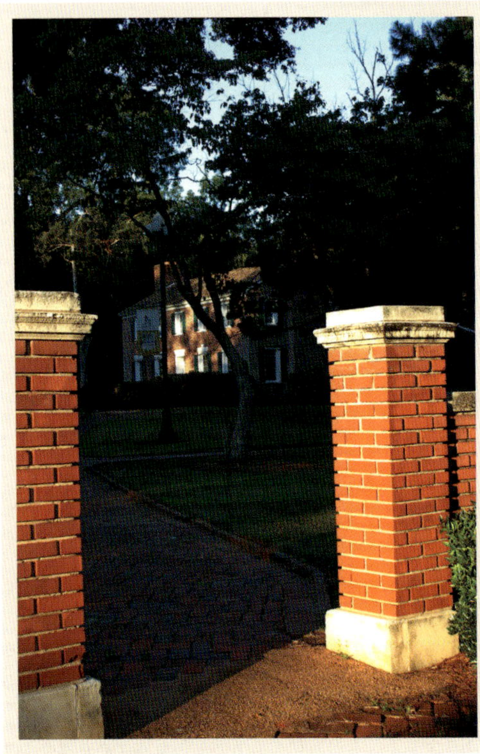

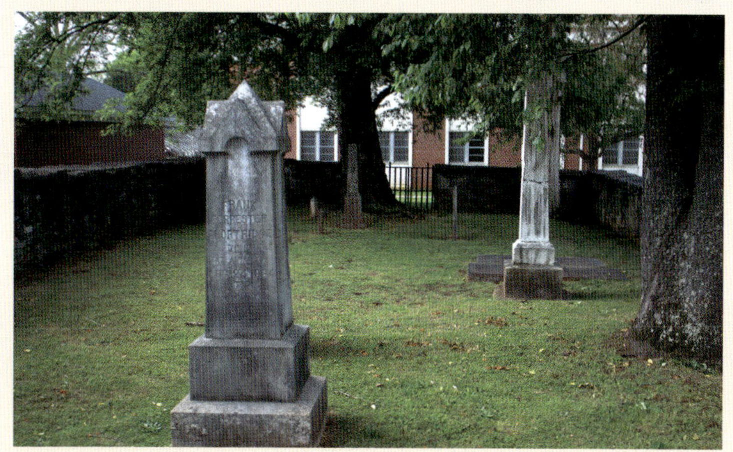

King Cemetery holds the graves of Edmund King; his wives Nancy, then Susan; and three sons, Nathaniel, Littleton, and Frank. Nathaniel accidentally shot and killed Littleton nearby in 1848. Frank King is buried next to his son, Morgan. Edmund and Nancy King's grandson George Shortridge Jr. returned home wounded from the Civil War. He did not recover and was buried in King Cemetery in 1868. The other marker serves as a memorial to family members buried elsewhere.

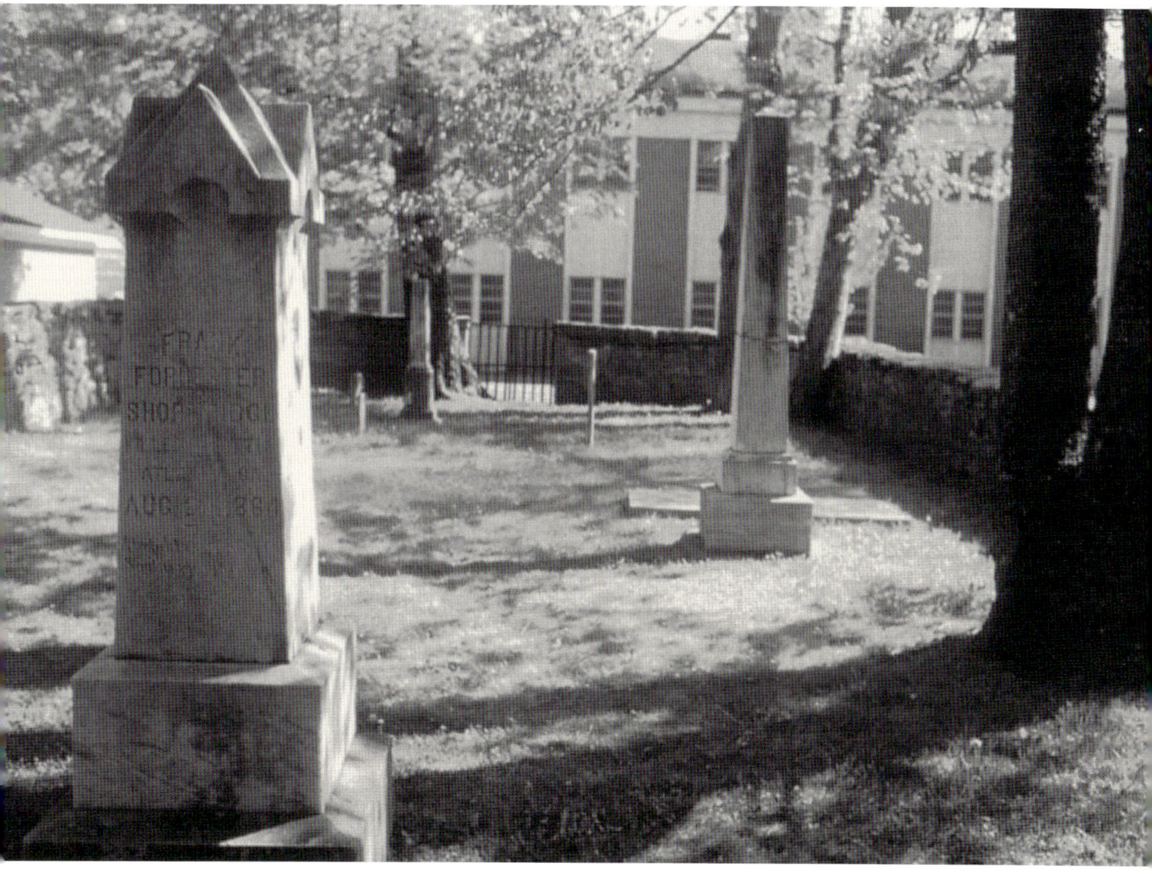

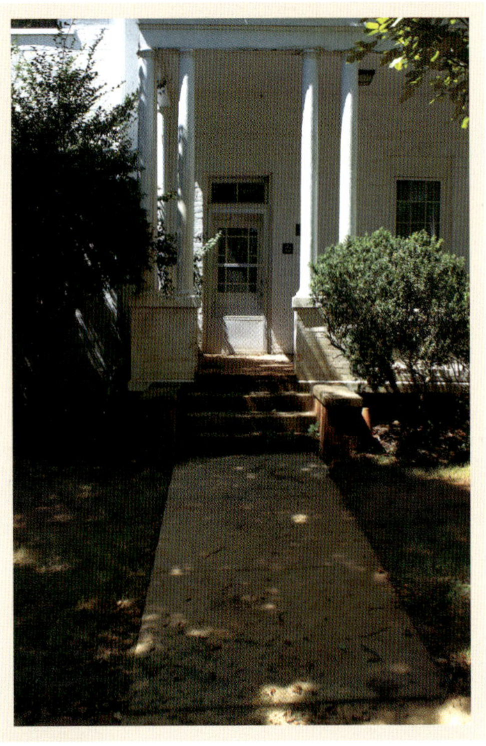

Lyman Hall (built in 1858), now Saylor House, is one of Montevallo's three antebellum campus structures. This Federal-style building served as the Montevallo Male and Female Institute, started by the Cumberland Presbyterian Church. The school did not survive the Civil War. Afterward, occupying Federal troops briefly used the structure. After Reconstruction, the Lyman family permitted educators to use parts of the home as classrooms and laboratory space. In 1952, the college purchased the building and named it after longtime nurse Edythe Saylor.

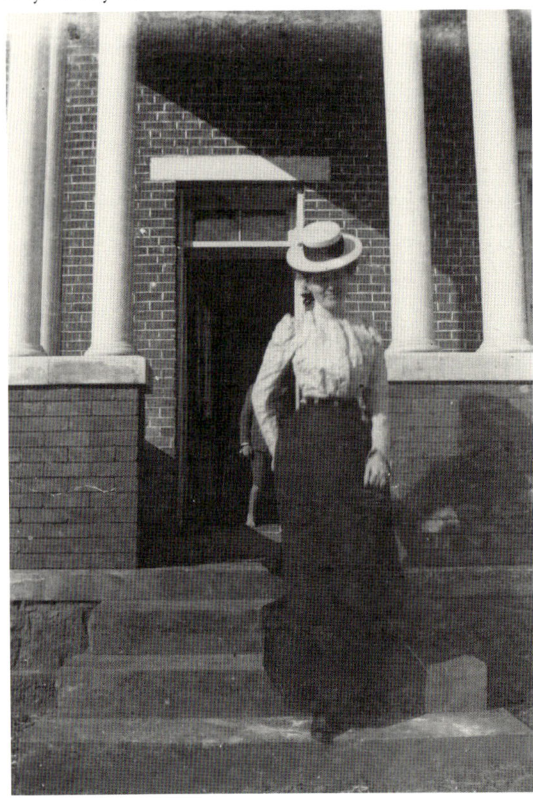

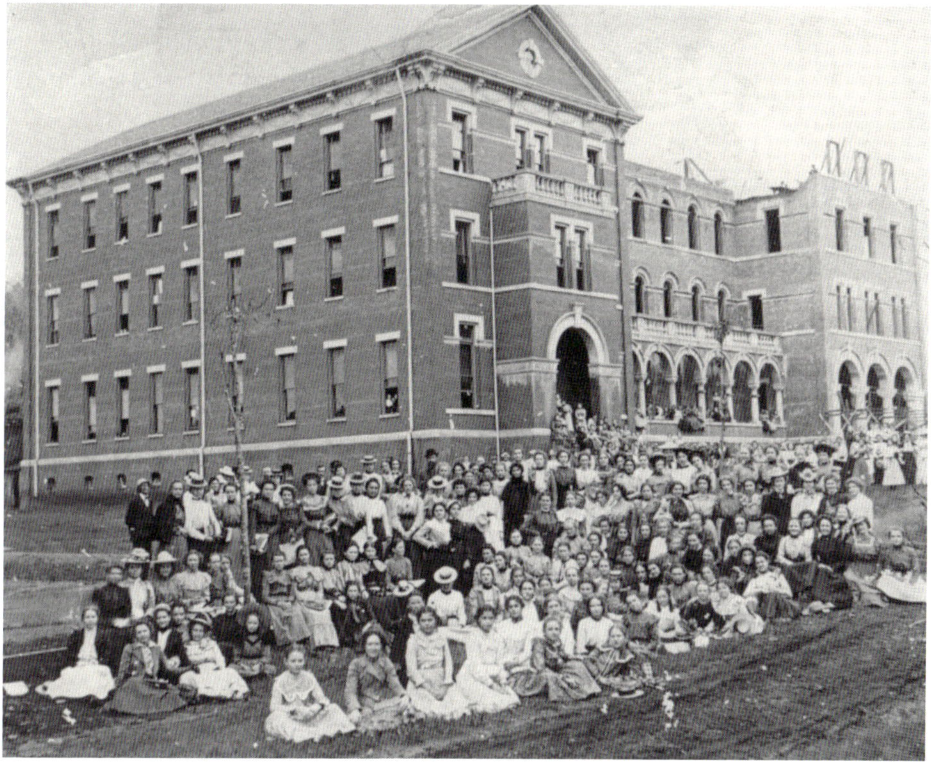

This c. 1900 image shows Main Hall dormitory under construction. The three wings are named after early faculty members: Elizabeth Haley, Anne E. Kennedy, and Mary Stallworth. The western portion, completed in 1897, housed 100 students. Soon after planning for the central wing, Main Hall began immediately to accommodate the growing student body featuring a new Otis elevator. The addition of a third wing in 1908 increased capacity to over 400 residents, and it remains the predominant structure on campus.

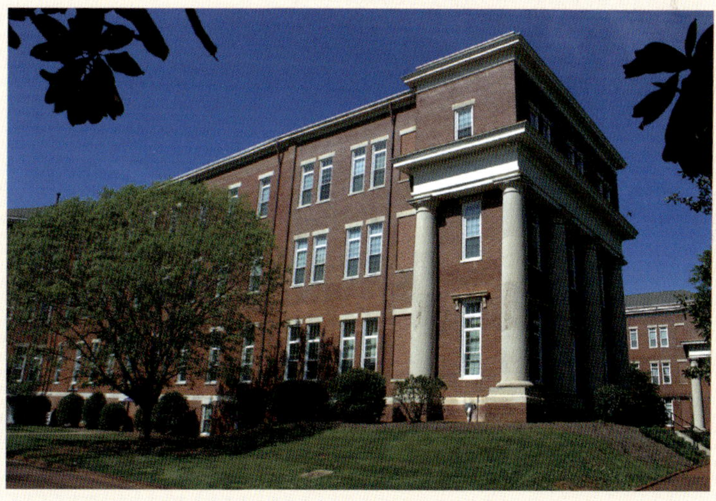

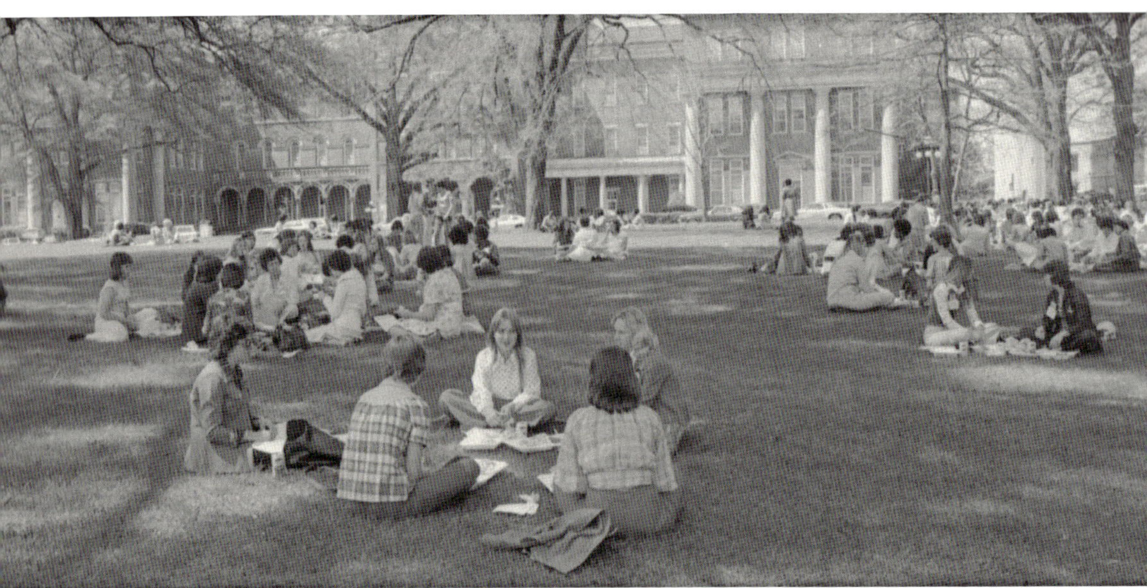

Situated near the original presidential residence, which burned in 1921 during Thomas Palmer's administration, *Becoming* offers an inspirational scene. Dedicated in 2003, the artwork represents the university's role in educating a student. The base represents the school's brick buildings, streets, and sidewalks. The larger hand represents the entire faculty and staff who endeavor to educate all aspects of a student's campus experience. The second hand represents the students and the transfer of knowledge.

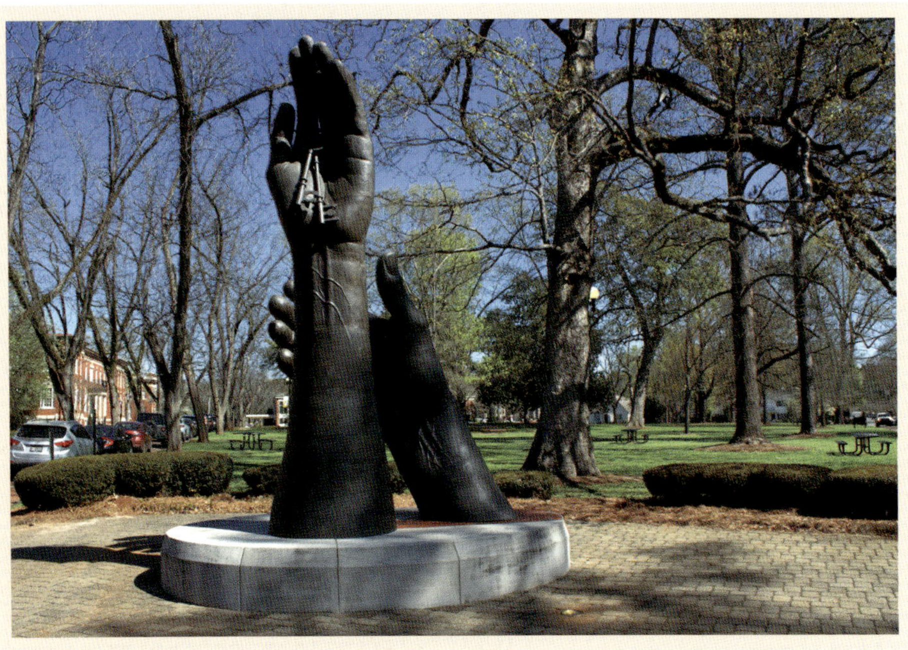

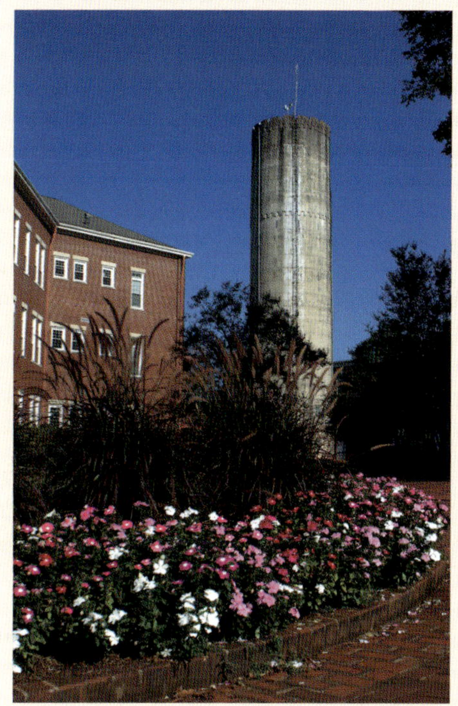

Completed in 1910, the Tower held a large reserve of water for the campus and the surrounding community. Transported to campus using early mechanical pumps, water traveled through a network of underground terra-cotta pipes from Big Springs, in modern-day Orr Park, and from Gentry Springs, located approximately three miles northwest of campus. The Tower now provides office space for Environmental Studies. The university named its literary magazine the *Tower* as an homage to the structure.

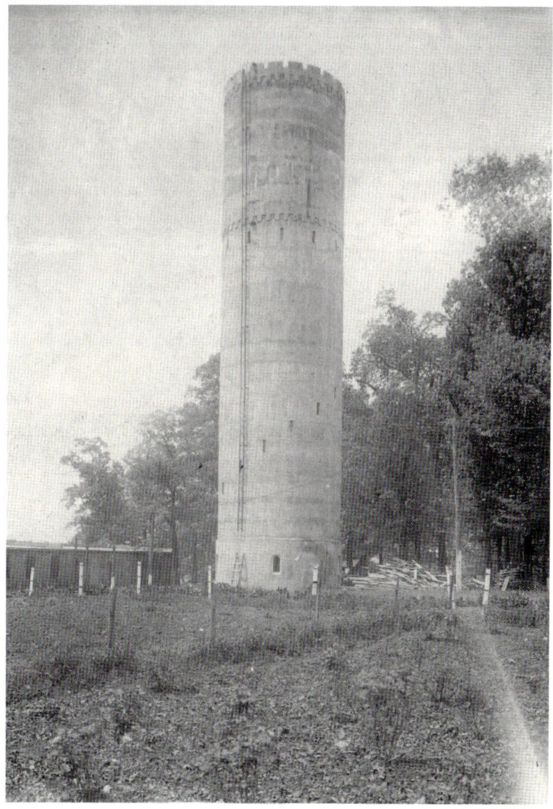

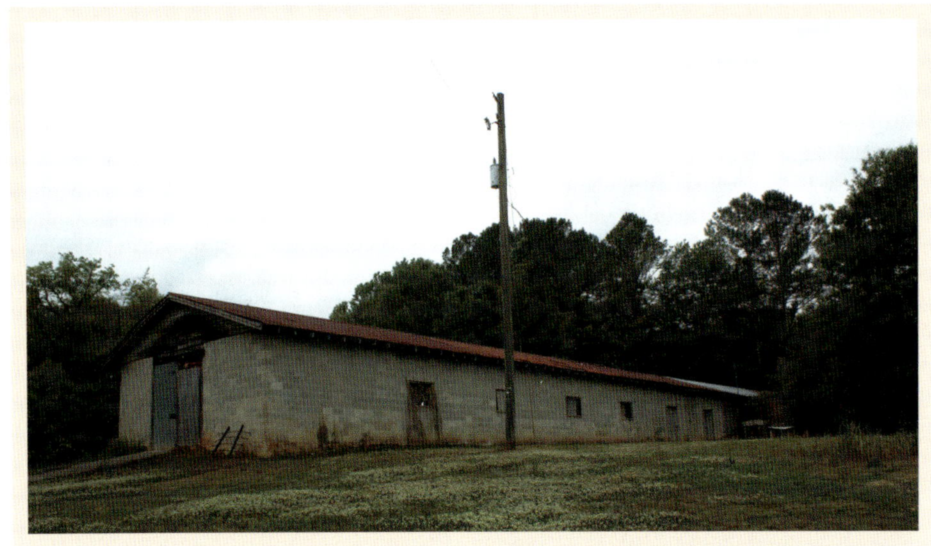

Due partly to food quality issues, by 1910, the Alabama Girls' Industrial School launched both a dairy and a farm to supply the school with the freshest possible nourishment. The dairy herd consisted of over 100 head of registered Holstein, Guernsey, and Jersey cattle. The farm also featured a piggery, ample gardens and orchards, and silage. For years, the school employed Samuel Chestnut, professor of science, to supervise dairy and farm practices. The school closed the operation in 1959.

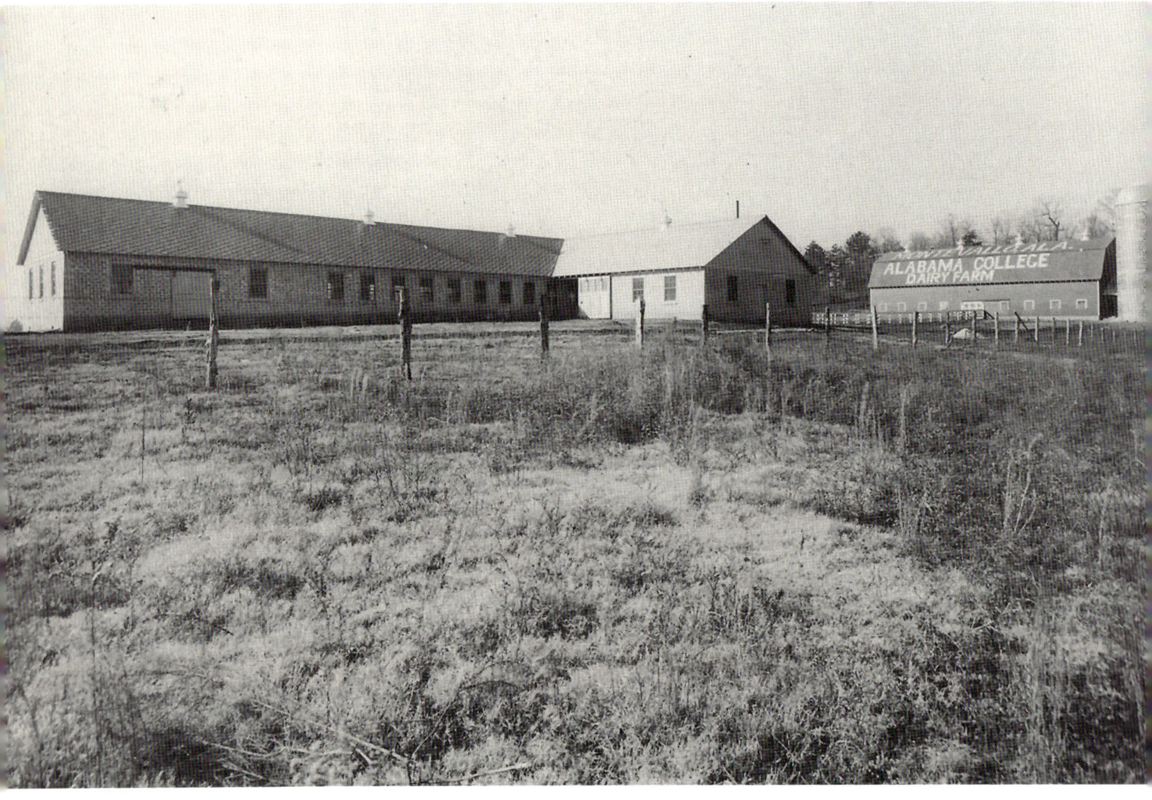

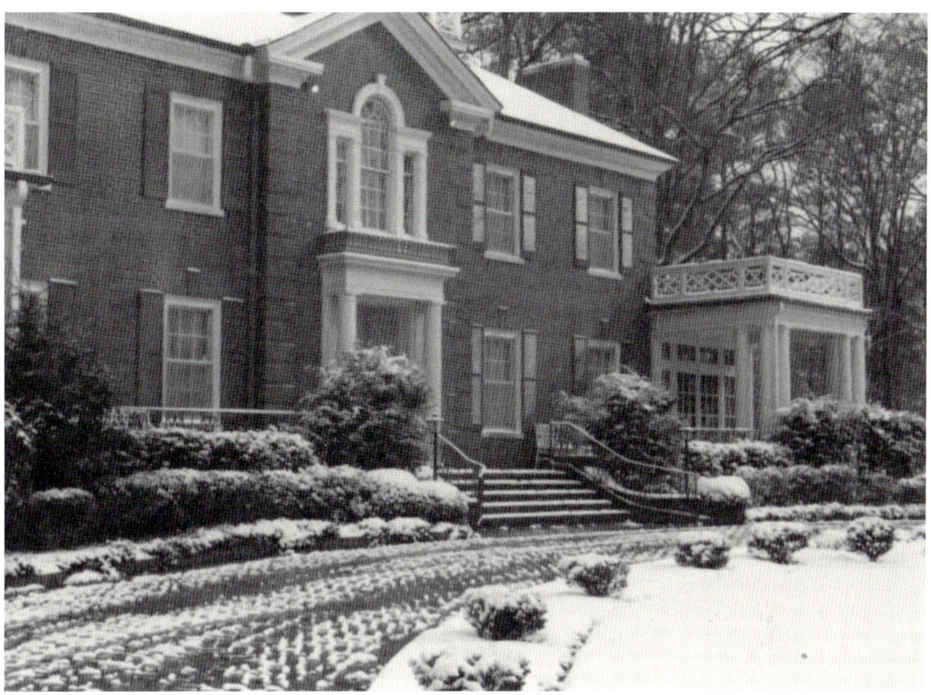

Starting with Oliver Cromwell Carmichael's administration in 1926, Flowerhill has served as the school's second presidential residence. Built to replace the original campus home destroyed by fire in 1921, the Flowerhill floor plan is a Sears, Roebuck & Co. kit home, the Magnolia. The front lawn features an amphitheater, built as a Works Progress Administration project in the 1930s, and a large quadrangle that has hosted spring commencement for over four decades.

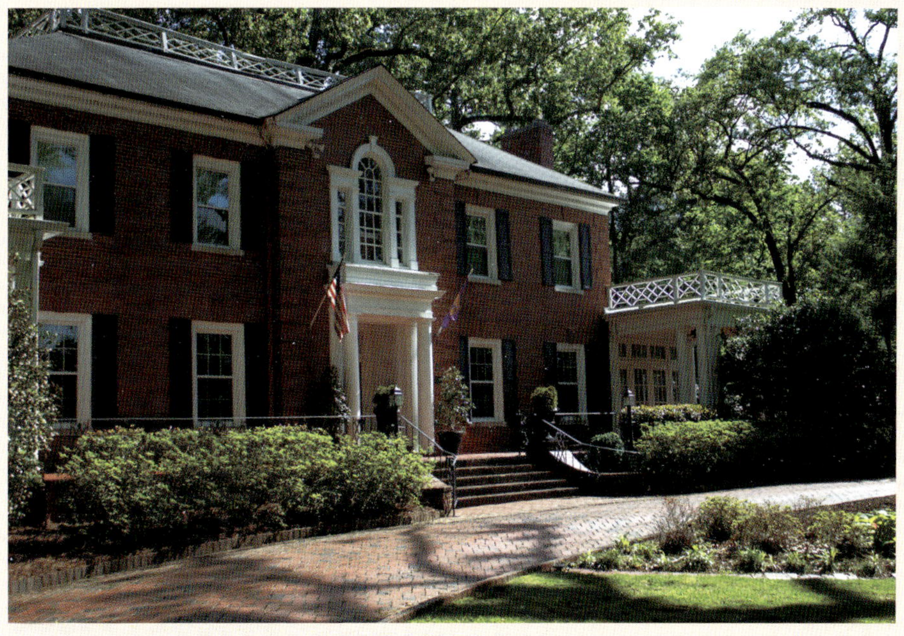

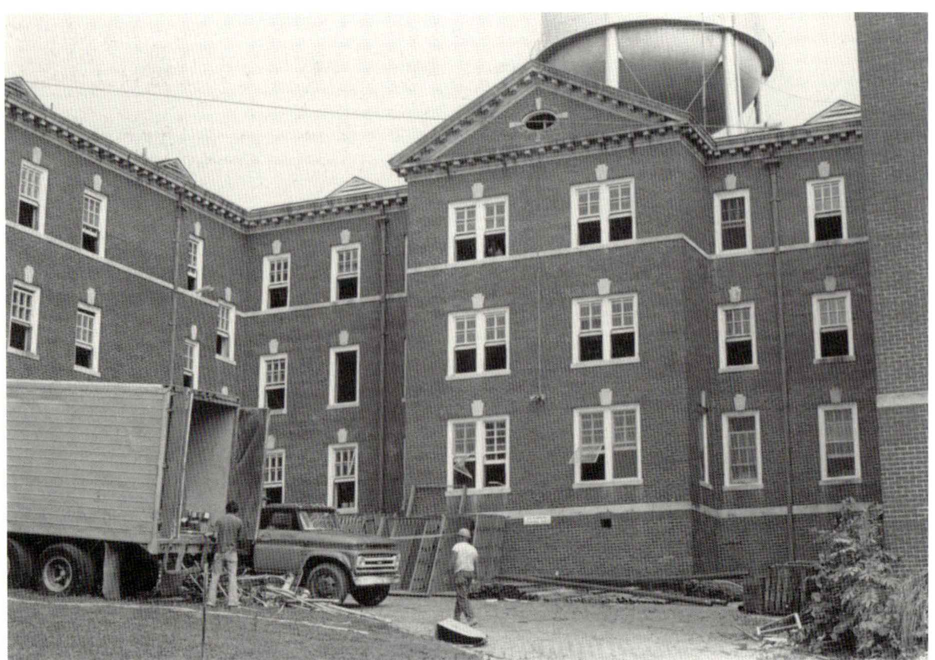

Funded by Alabama College's first fundraising campaign in 1925, Janet Erskine Ramsay Hall became the second campus residence hall. Designed by the firm of Warren, Knight, and Davis, the dormitory provided 200 rooms each featuring built-in vanities and closets. A 1979 building renovation transformed it into a conference center. In 2015, most of the hotel rooms returned to student use. Today, the ground floor houses the dean of the College of Arts & Sciences and the Honors Program.

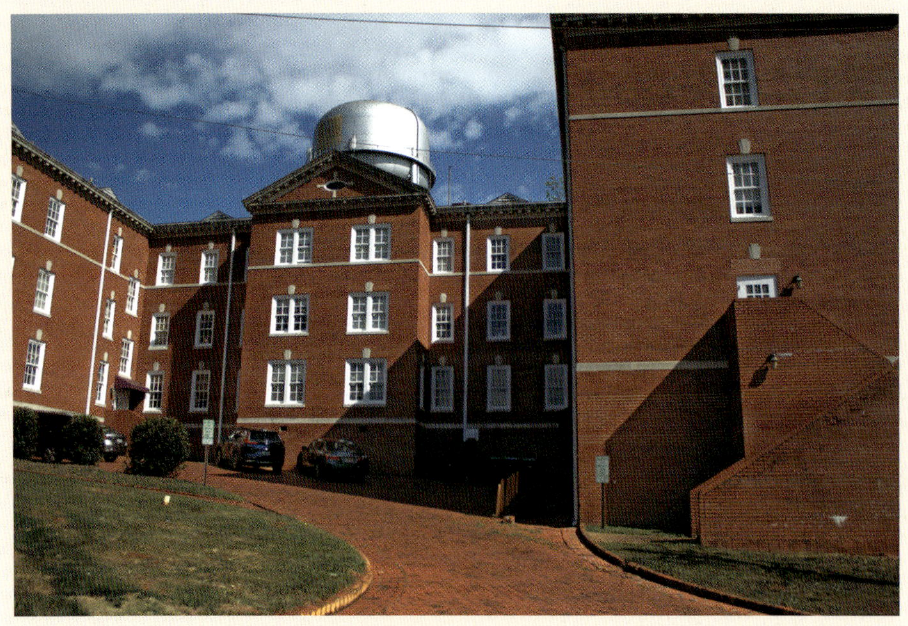

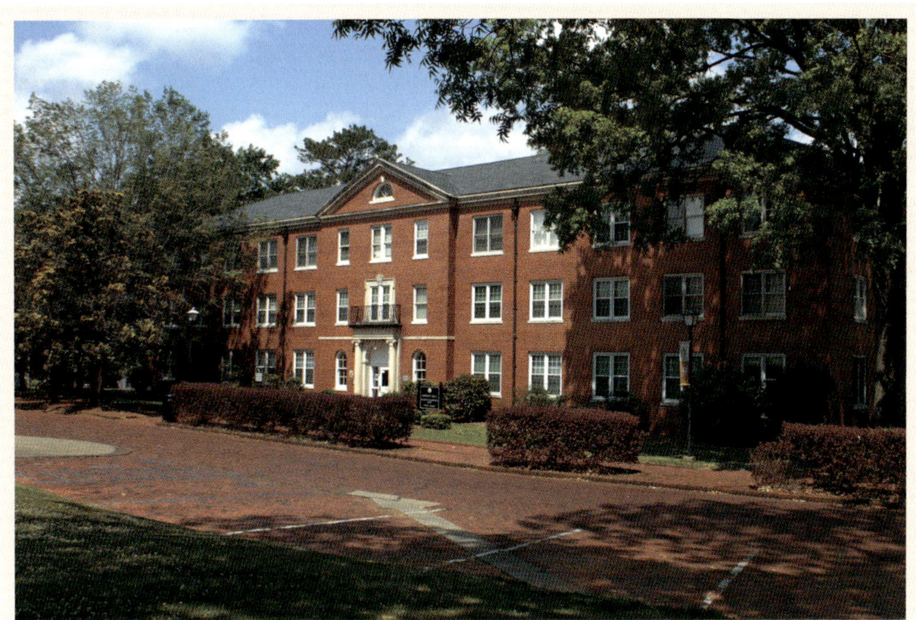

Completed in 1929, Wenona Hanson Hall offered expanded residential options for campus. It was built for over $140,000 with state government funds heavily supplemented by Victor Hanson, proprietor of the *Birmingham News* newspaper. The hall features 96 rooms and houses about 192 women. The building is named for Hanson's wife, the former Wenona White, a Montgomery schoolteacher and conservatory-trained musician.

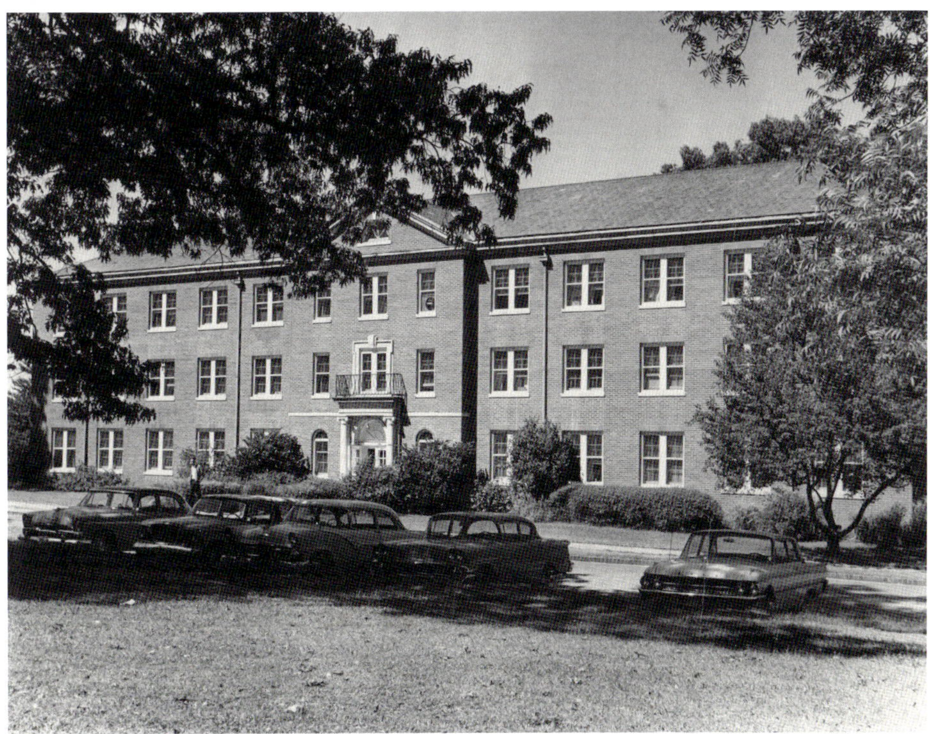

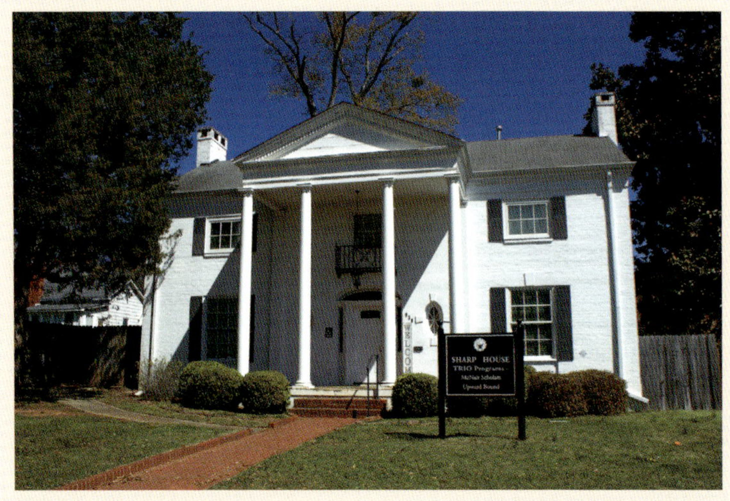

Dr. Cleveland G. Sharp, professor of biology at Alabama College for 38 years and departmental chair, built a Greek Revival home directly adjacent to campus. He also served on Montevallo's city council as mayor from 1944 to 1952. The home, known then as the Sharp House, was later converted to apartments and then housed the Alpha Tau Omega fraternity. In 2014, the university obtained the building for administrative purposes and restored the name to the Sharp House.

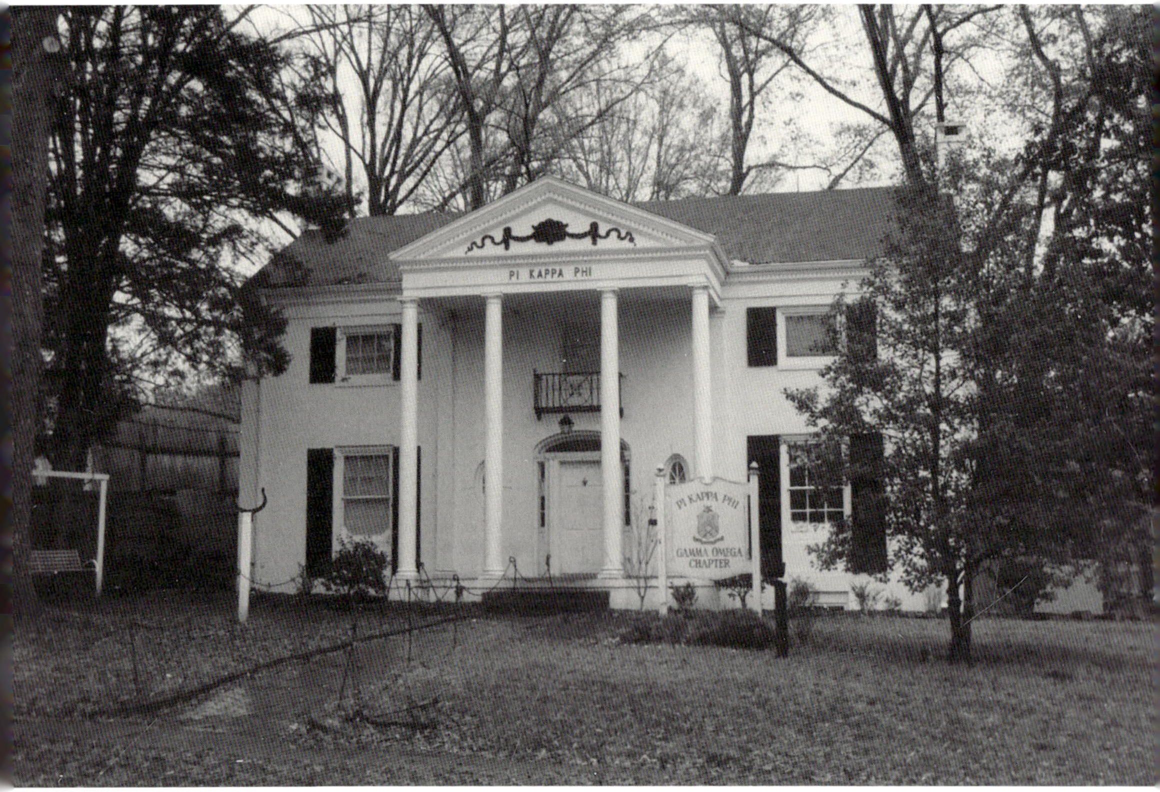

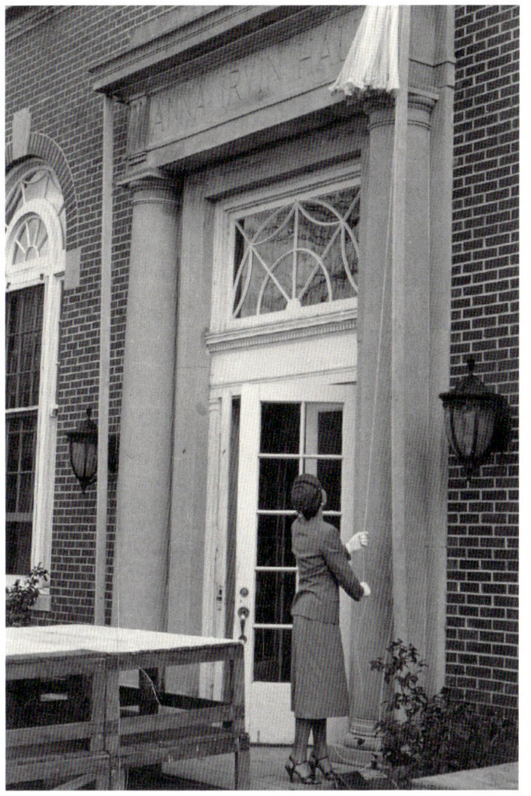

Alabama College's dining hall, in the basement of Main Hall, became inadequate to serve the school's growing population, resulting in the construction of Anna Irvin Hall in 1929. With the admission of male students, dining transitioned from family style to cafeteria style. The school upgraded the Anna Irvin kitchen and expanded the building in the 1970s to meet campus demands. Today's dining hall features the Executive Dining Room and the Montevallo Room, offering space for formal gatherings.

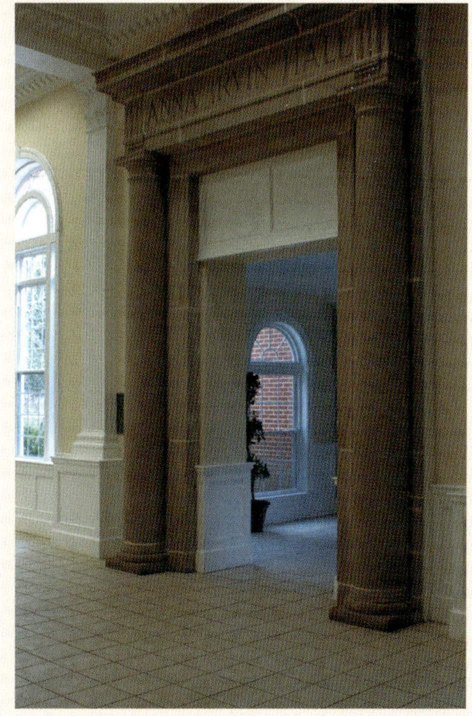

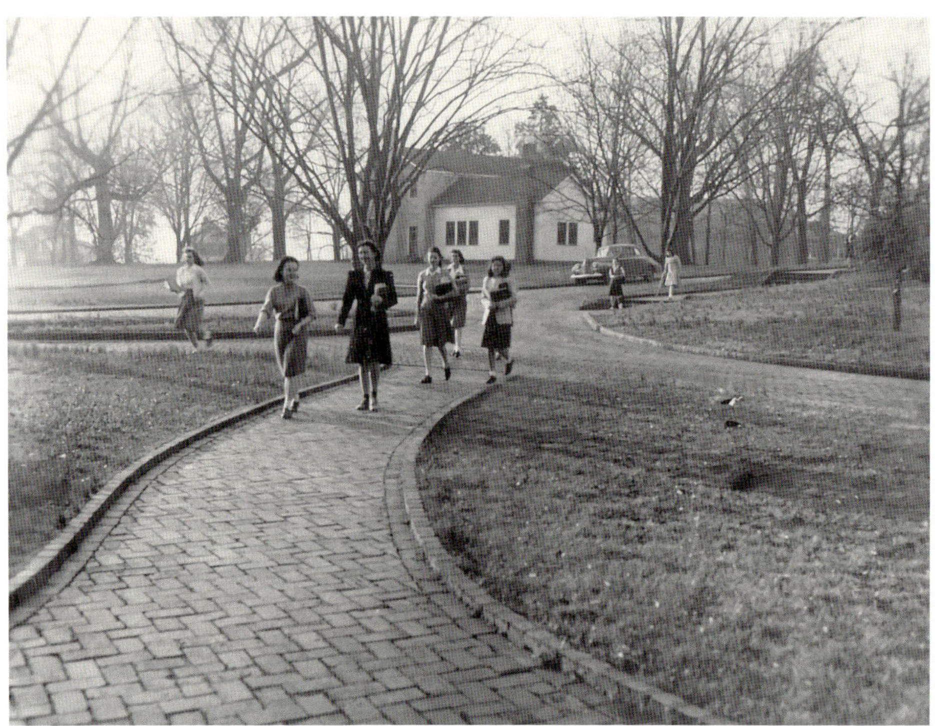

In the late 1920s, the Olmsted Brothers firm of Brookline, Massachusetts, featured bricks as the centerpiece of its Alabama College landscape architectural plan, giving the campus its iconic streets and sidewalks. These images show King-Harman Street, perhaps the busiest street on campus in terms of foot traffic. King House sits in the background. The university secured a bond issue in 2012, and under the then-director of the Physical Plant, Billy Hughes, brick restoration projects occurred across campus, including saving a vintage amphitheater.

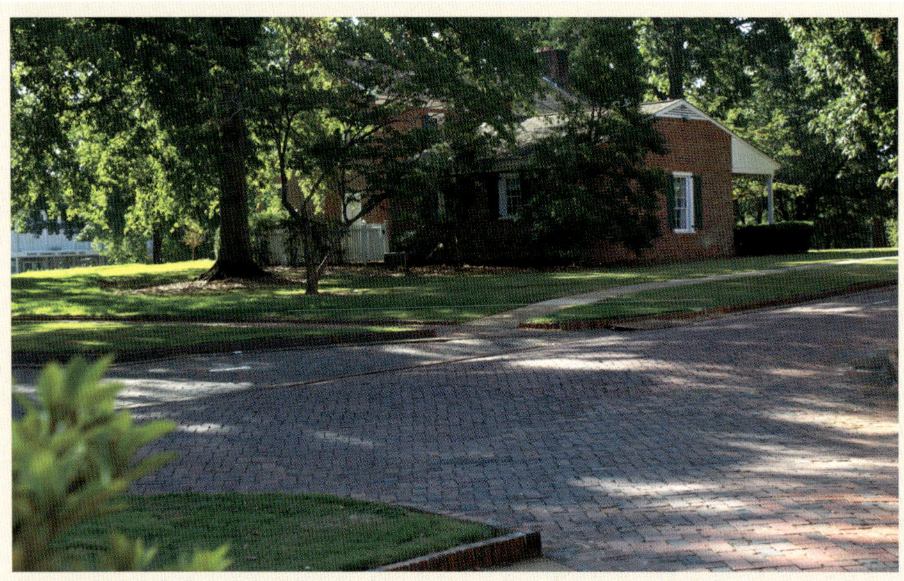

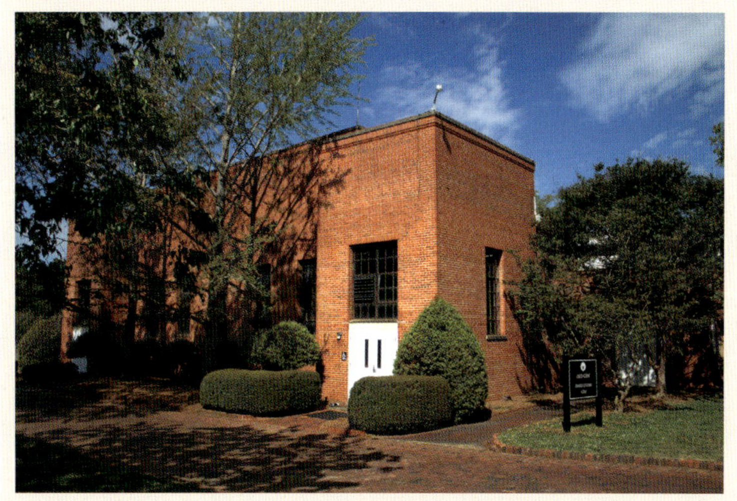

The field house formerly known as Bibb Graves Hall and now known as the Old Gym was originally intended as an airport hangar during the 1930s. However, the Works Progress Administration abandoned this plan, and it became Alabama College's athletics facility. With the completion of Myrick Gymnasium in the 1970s, the Old Gym became a practice facility and community exercise center. In recent years, the building has undergone restoration and served as the home of Montevallo's esports program from 2019 to 2021.

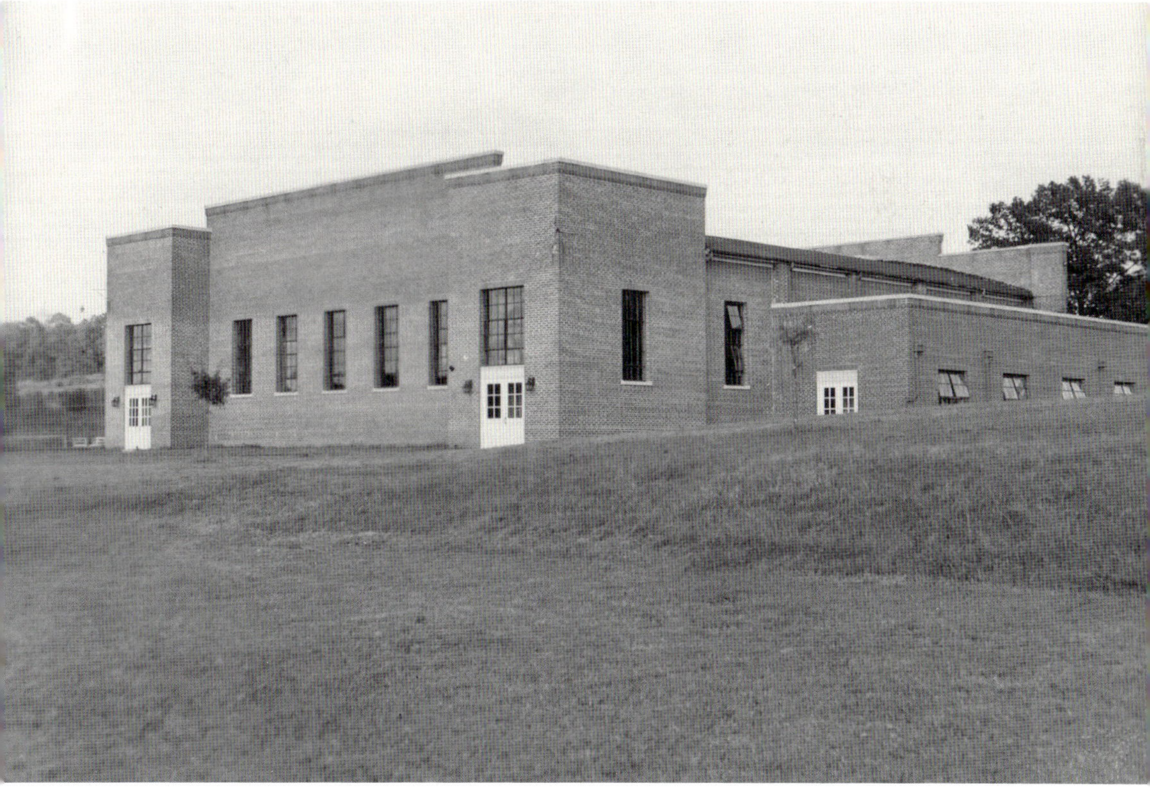

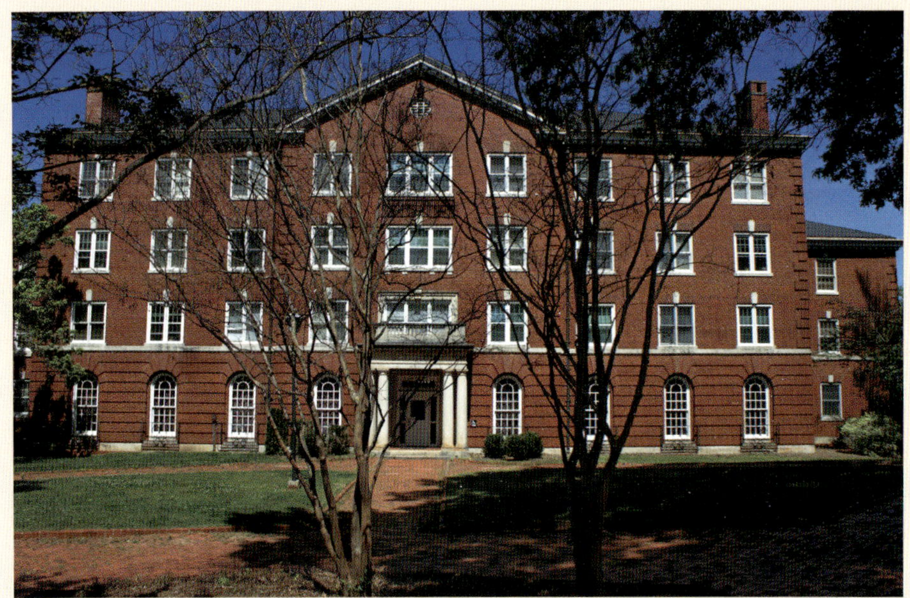

Julia Tutwiler (1841–1916), an advocate for women's education, was one of the first inductees into the Alabama Women's Hall of Fame. Initially named as the first president of the Alabama Girls' Industrial School, she resigned due to disagreements over insufficient state appropriations for the institution. With Works Progress Administration funds in the late 1930s, Alabama College constructed Tutwiler Hall as the senior dormitory in her honor. Called "Tut" by its residents, the building now houses all classes of female students.

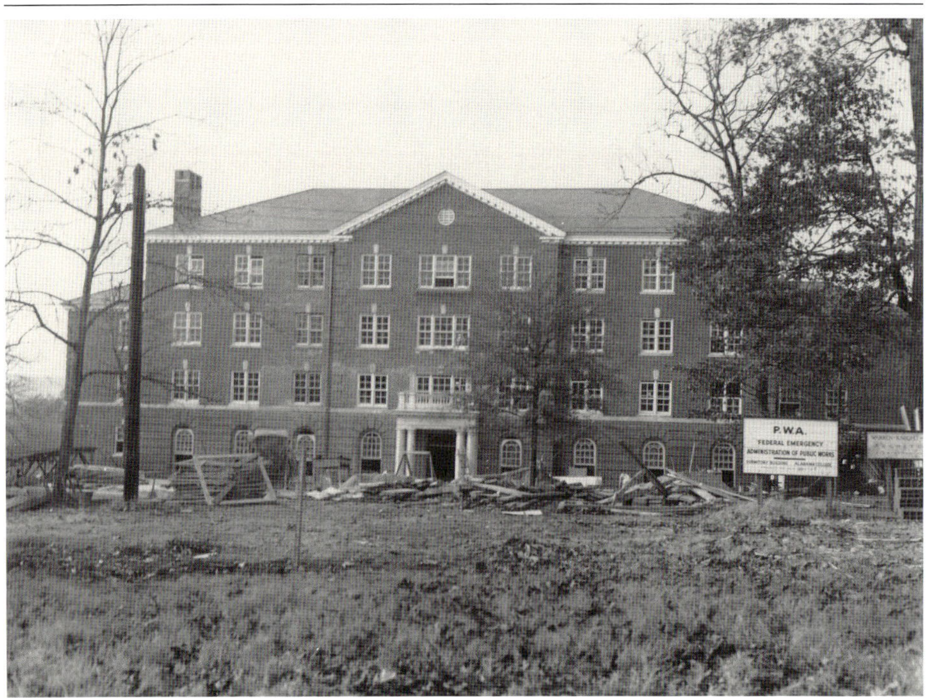

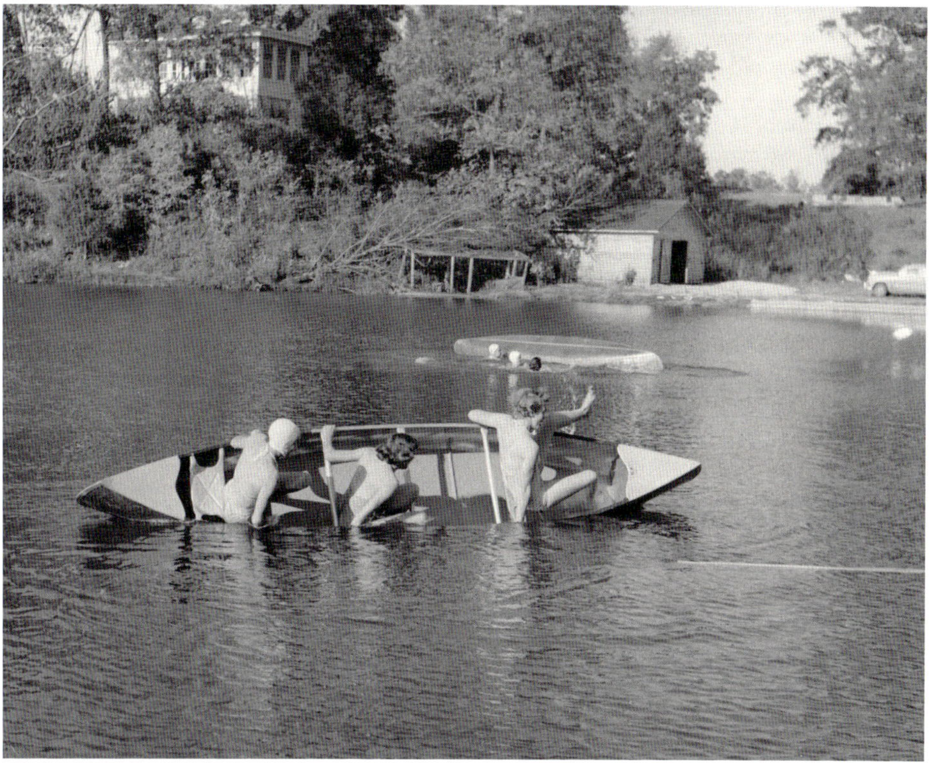

Announced in 1950 and completed in 1951, the college constructed a 12-acre lake on the grounds of a meadow adjacent to the school's camphouse. Today, the University Lake, a half mile from campus, provides extra recreation and possibilities for physical education courses with boating, swimming, and fishing. The grounds include a modest faculty house with a screened-in porch and a kitchen. In 2021, the university opened the Walden Studio, based on the cabin of Henry David Thoreau.

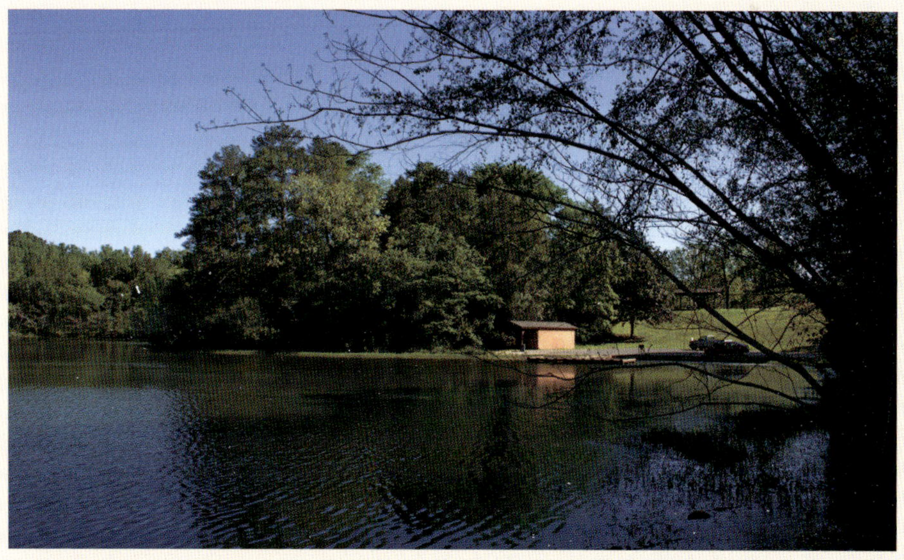

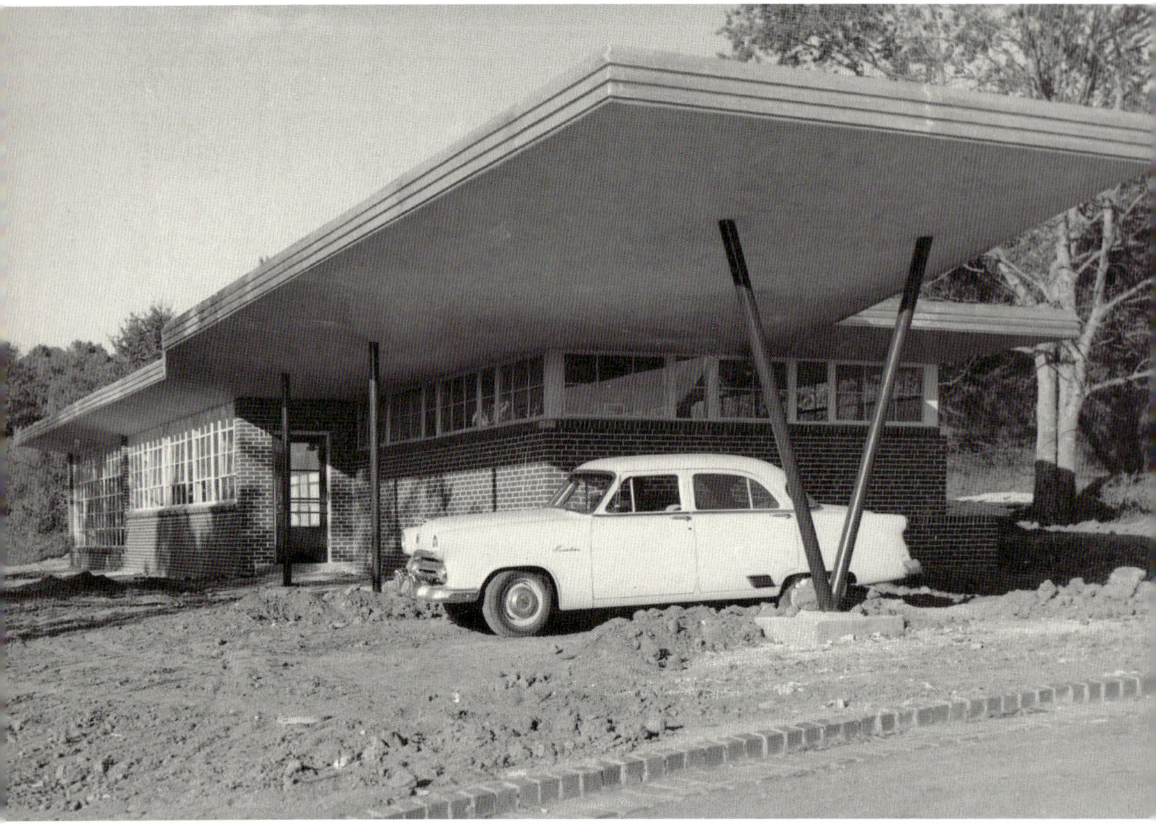

In 1931, Dr. Dura-Louise Cockrell of the Department of Home Economics launched a nursery school for Alabama College. The structure, a small frame house, stood where Carmichael Library is today. In 1955, the school upgraded the facilities with a brand-new building known as the Child Study Center adjacent to what is today Strong Hall. The center engages children with a "creative curriculum" and stresses hands-on learning and authentic experiences. Many current faculty and staff enroll their children here.

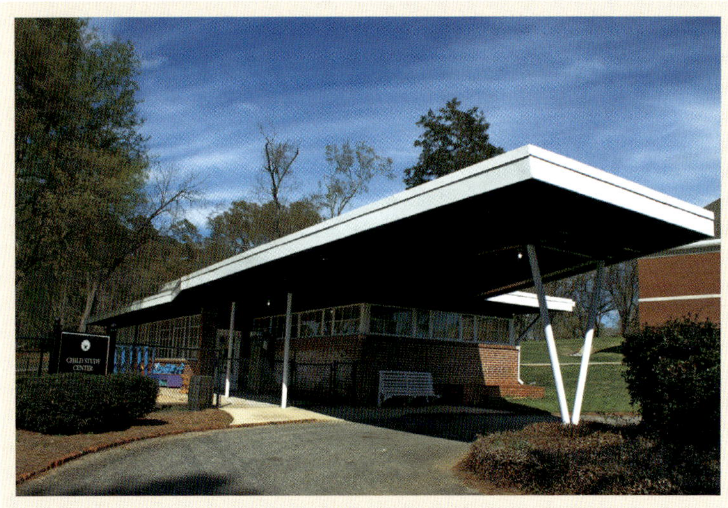

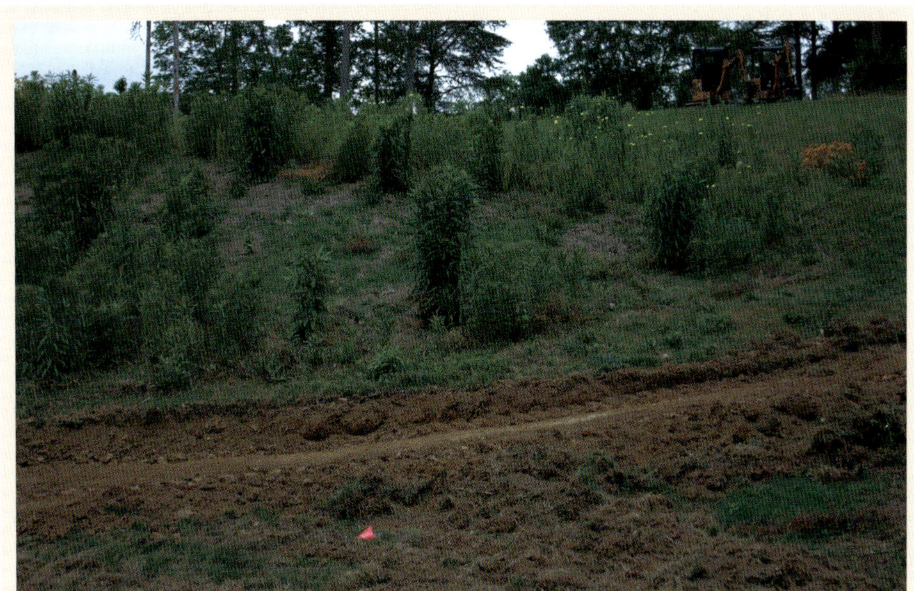

The Montevallo Golf Course opened in 1957 adjacent to the College Lake. While the course belongs to the university, the city operated it for decades. The school's men's golf team played its inaugural season in 1960, and the women's team followed in 1995. Today, both golf teams play home matches at Timberline Golf Course in Calera. The university began to repurpose the golf course for the school's new mountain biking team in 2023.

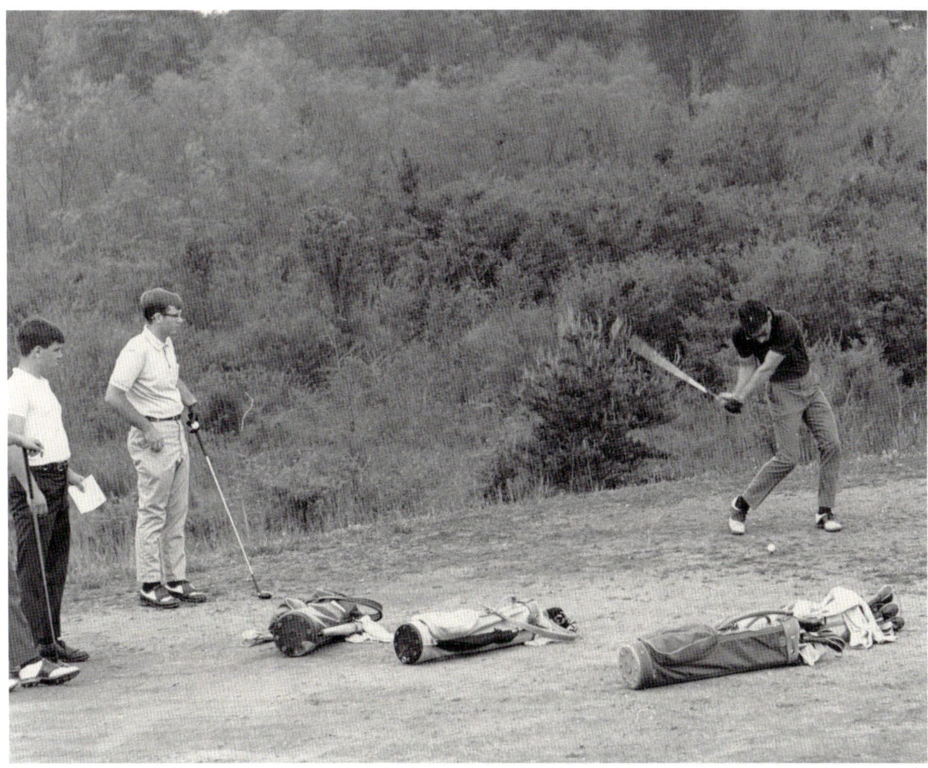

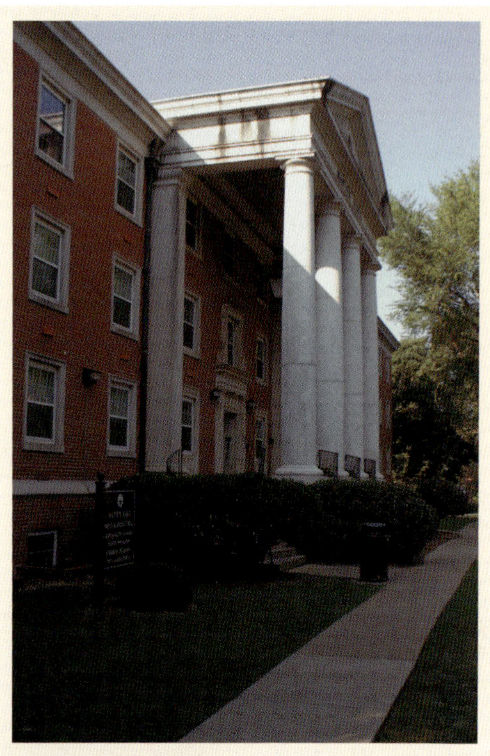

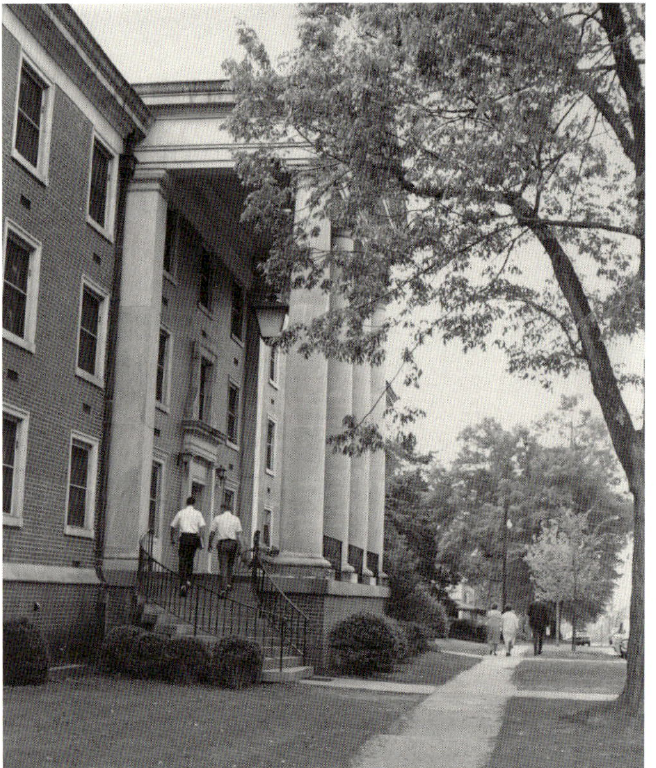

Opened in 1957 and named for long-serving and beloved dean Thomas H. Napier, Napier Hall allowed men to be centrally housed on campus. Dean Napier and his wife, Mary, hosted lavish end-of-the-year teas for graduating seniors. Prior to becoming officially coeducational in 1956, Alabama College let men attend special sessions and accommodated returning soldiers under the GI Bill. Previously male students lived in King House, in a section of Main Hall, or found lodgings elsewhere until 1957.

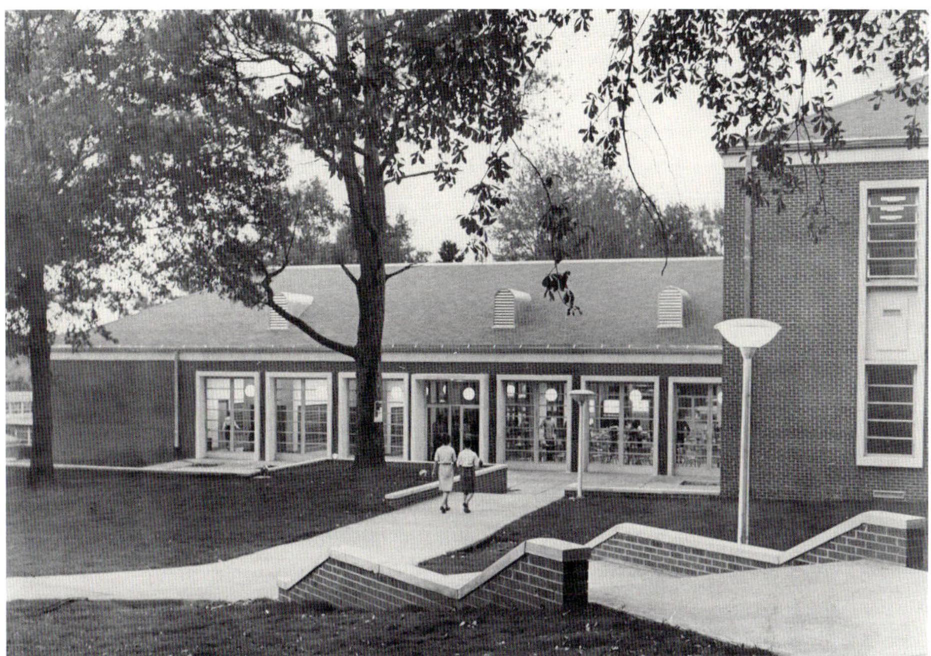

With rapid student growth in the 1960s, the school constructed a new student union building, Farmer Hall, named after longtime history professor and social activist Dr. Hallie Farmer. The "SUB," as it was called, housed the bookstore, student government offices, the post office, and a two-lane bowling alley. The university renovated the building on two separate occasions, most recently in 2014. On Founders' Day in 2022, the university dedicated the post office to Charlie Webb Jr., the campus mail carrier.

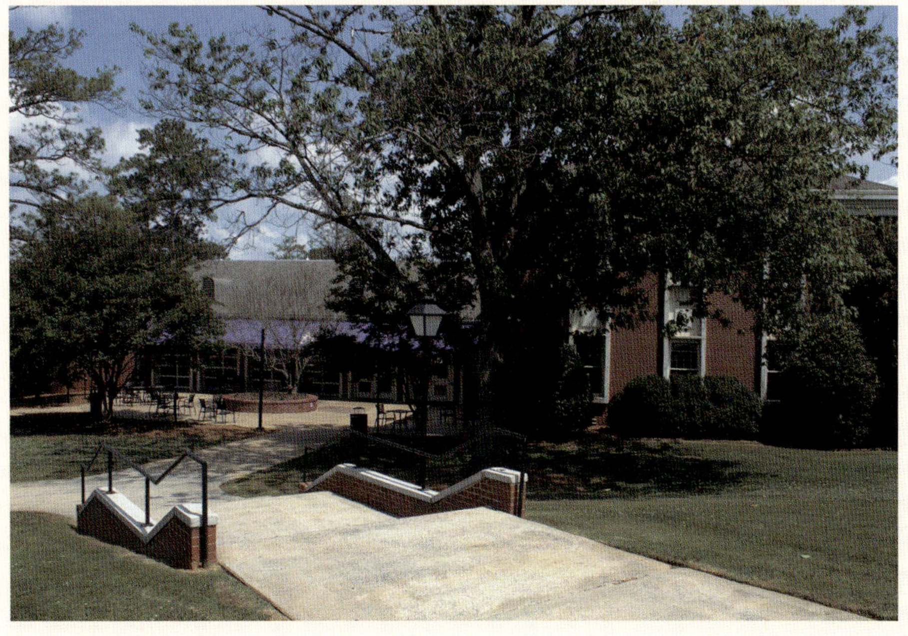

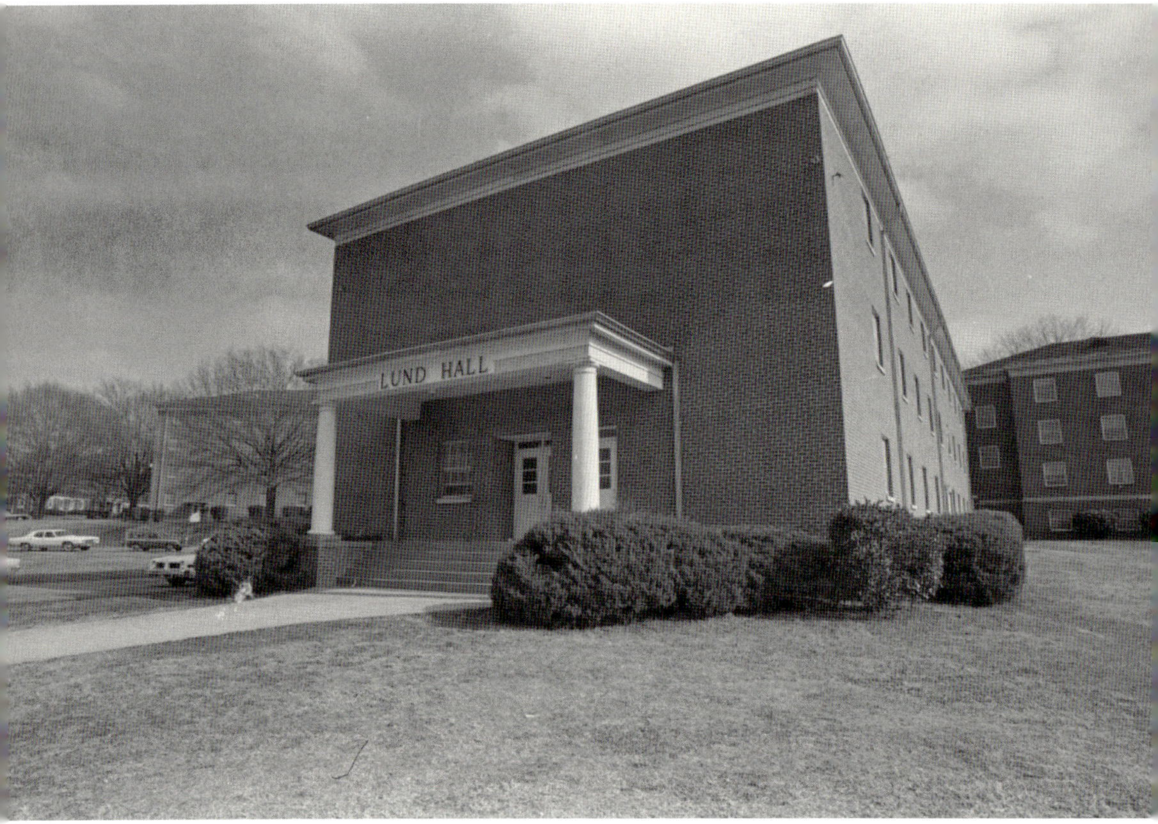

Franz Edward Lund was president of Alabama College from 1952 to 1957, during an era of shrinking enrollments and challenging financial conditions. He grew the school with both a graduate program and the official entrance of male students in 1956. With the rapid increase of students in the 1960s, the university built new dormitories including Lund Hall, named in his honor in 1969. The building housed over 100 students. One can note the now-demolished Fuller Hall in this 1970s photograph.

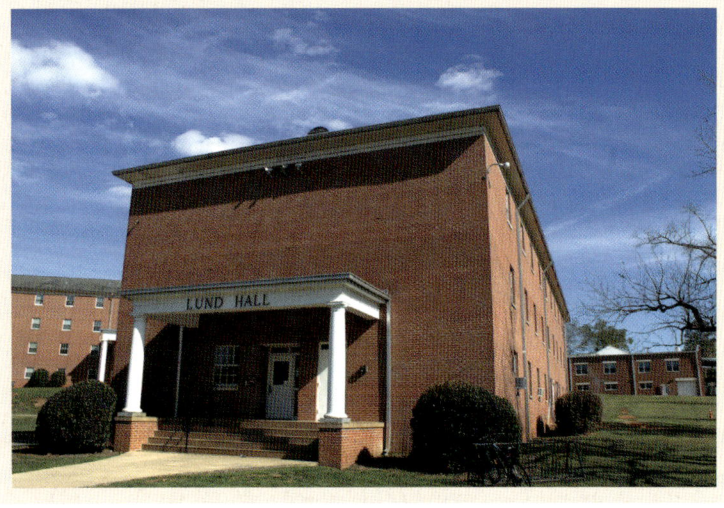

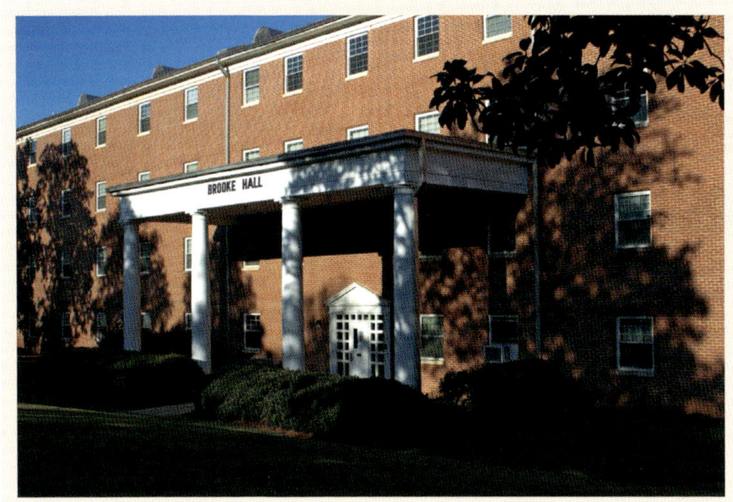

During the rapid expansion of the 1960s, the school erected new dormitories, including Brooke Hall (built in 1969). The dormitory housed over 200 women and a house director, and each room had a private bath. In 1978, the university dedicated the building to Myrtle Brooke. Brooke taught various courses in social sciences, but she is best known for creating the social work program in 1925, one of the oldest in the Southeast. Today, Chi Omega has its residency in the building.

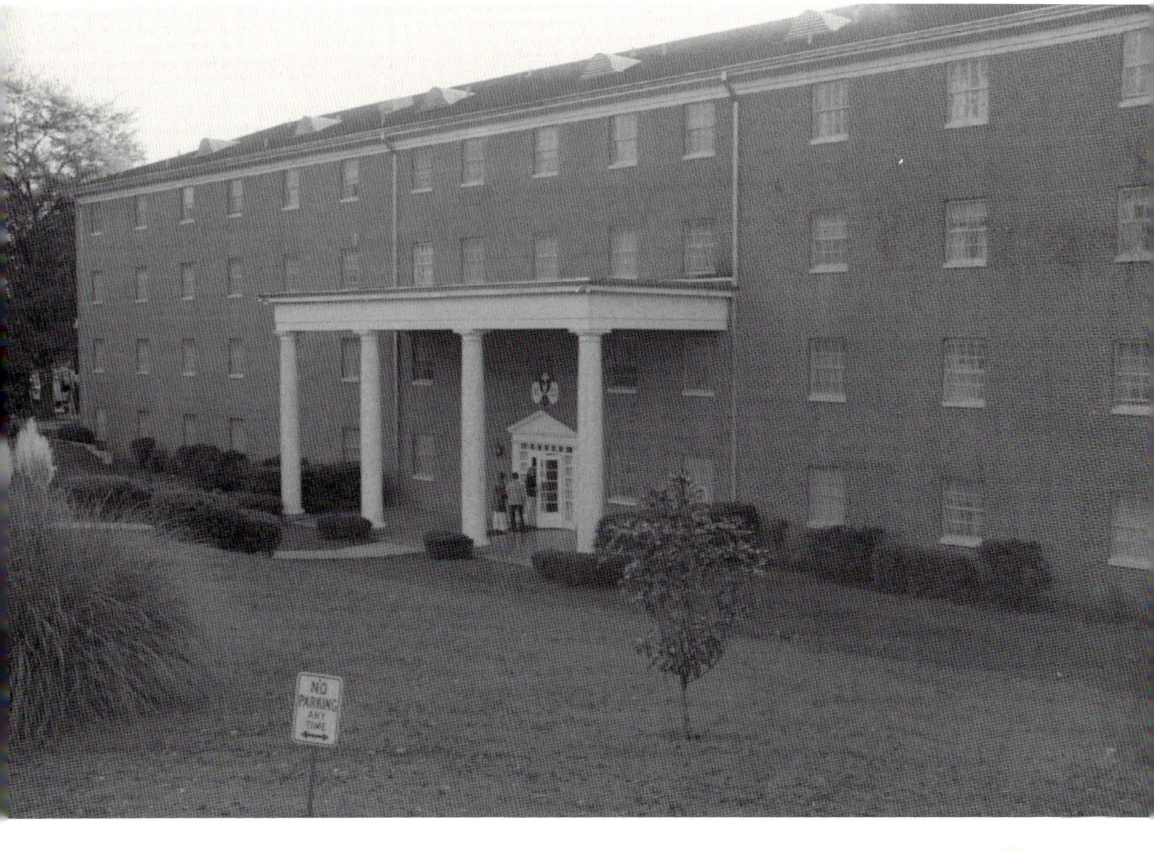

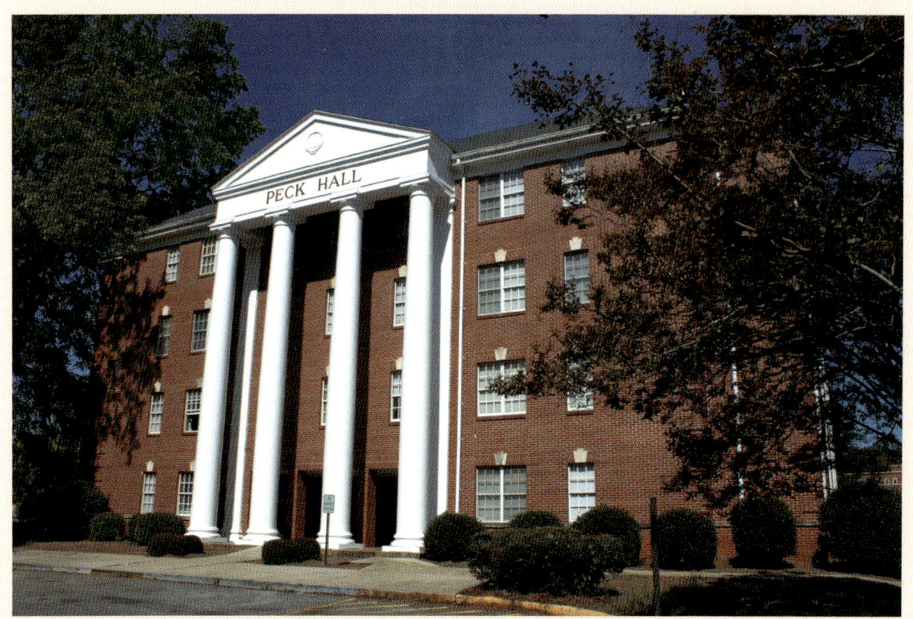

The school named Peck Hall after the first full-time doctor of the campus, Dr. Willena Peck. It functioned as the school's first coeducational apartment building, with individual rooms, baths, and kitchens. In 1915, Dr. Peck succeeded Dr. D.L. Wilkerson, who had served as a part-time physician and who protested Peck's appointment over him. Dr. Peck lived on campus in the Peterson Infirmary and served the institution faithfully until her retirement in 1952.

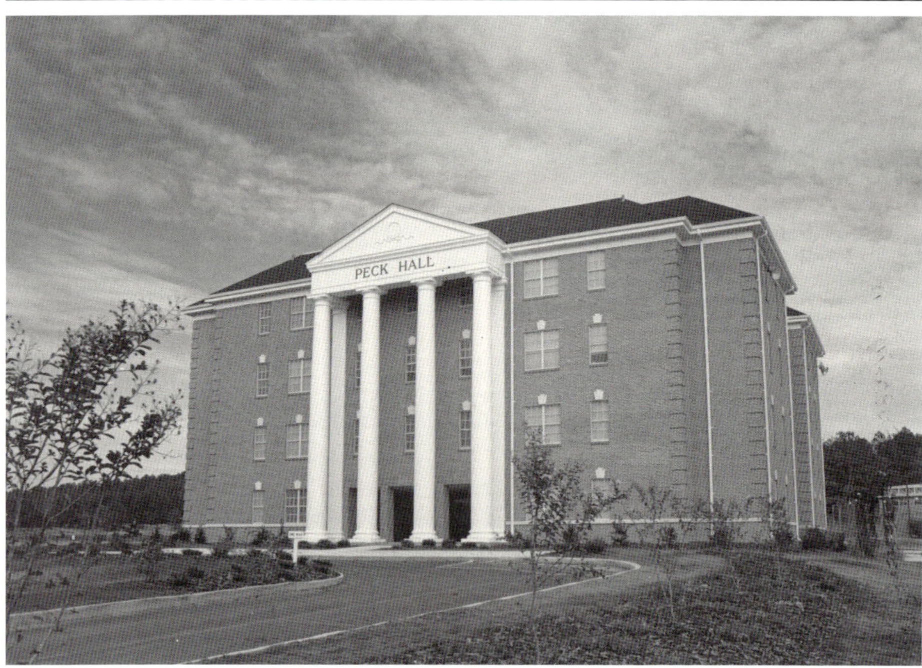

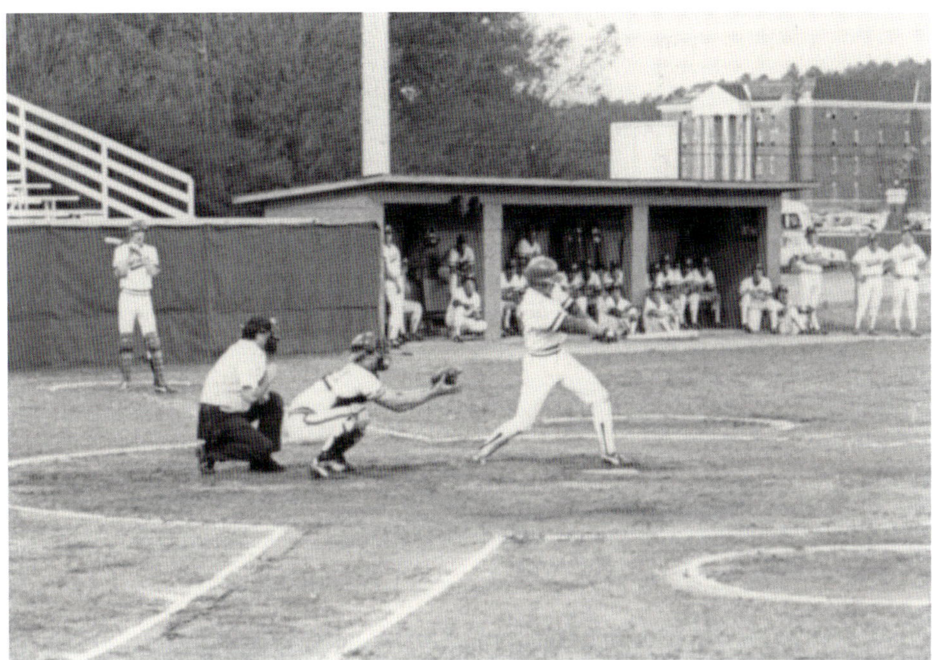

Sports have played a significant role in university history. In 1958, baseball became the school's first National Collegiate Athletic Association–recognized sport. The team initially played on a crude field with concrete-block dugouts until it built a proper space. In 1981, the school improved its baseball facility and named it in honor of Dr. Kermit A. Johnson, who served as University of Montevallo president from 1968 to 1977. The university has upgraded Kermit Johnson Field in phases over the last 20 years.

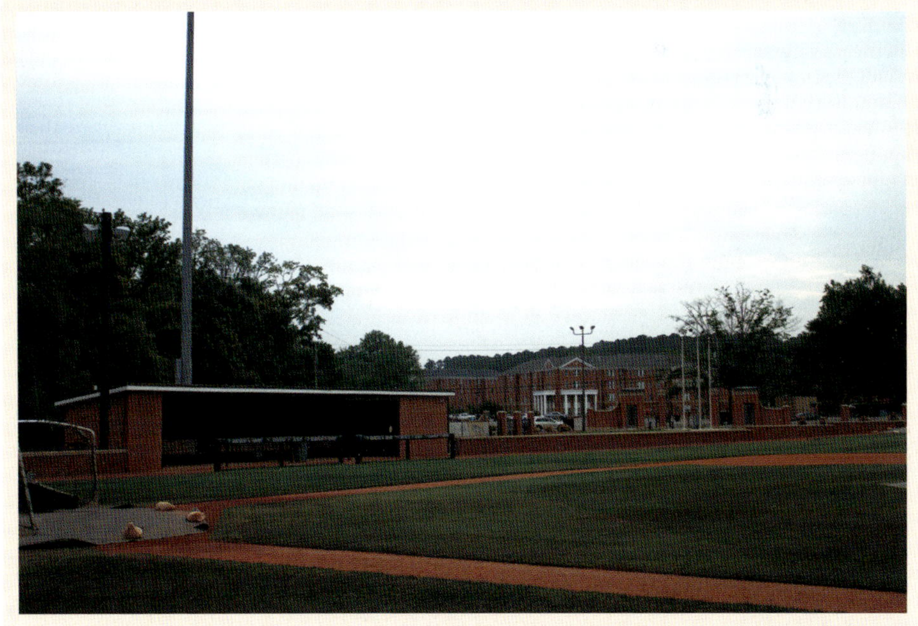

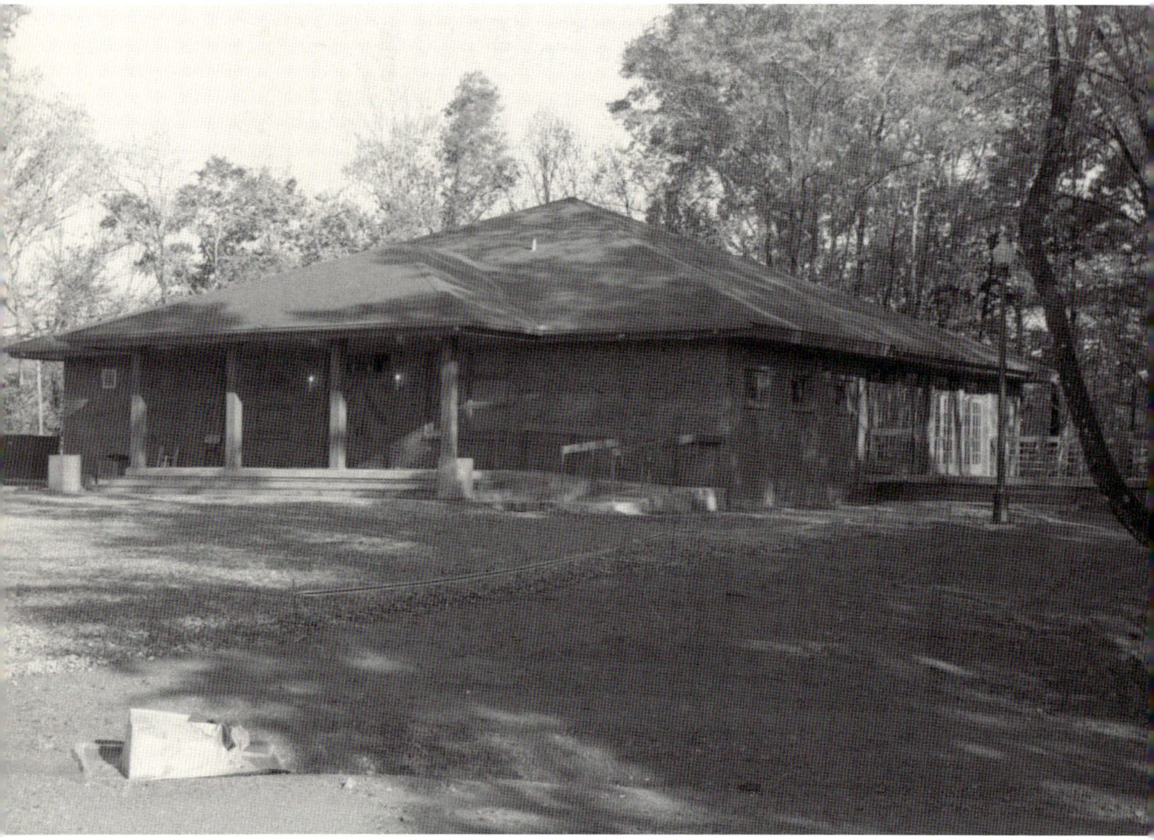

The condemnation of the Lake House at the University Lake saw students without a site for social gatherings on or near campus. Under then-president John W. Stewart in 1991, the university built and unveiled a lodge-style building on a rustic tree-encircled site. The facility has a small kitchen, bar, and sound system for conferences, presentations, and student organizations. Students proposed that the structure would bear Stewart's name.

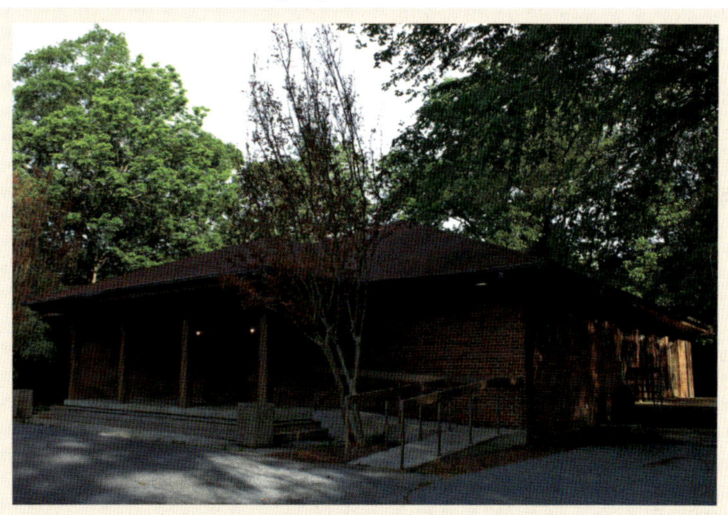

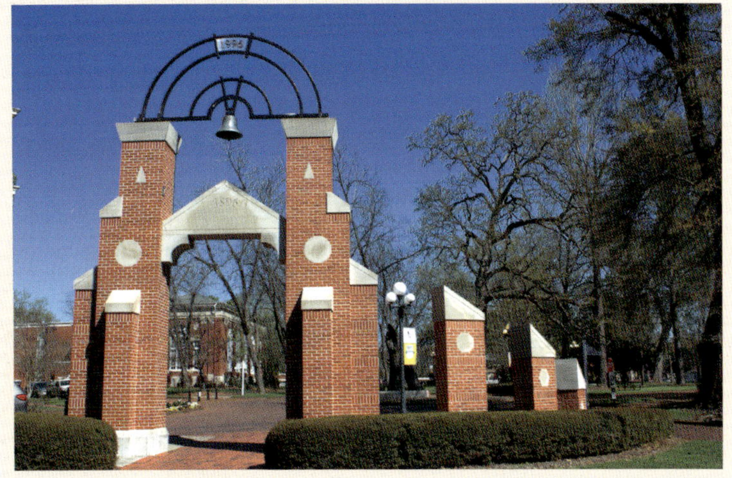

Named for donors Sandra Bond Bowers, class of 1966, and Richard Bowers, the Bowers Colonnade stands on Main Quad near Main Hall and *Becoming*. The colonnade represents the steps students ascend each year. The school symbolically welcomes seniors to their last undergraduate year as the bell rings once for every year of the institution's existence as they process into Palmer Auditorium for the annual Founders' Day celebration. This 1978 image shows students relaxing at its current location.

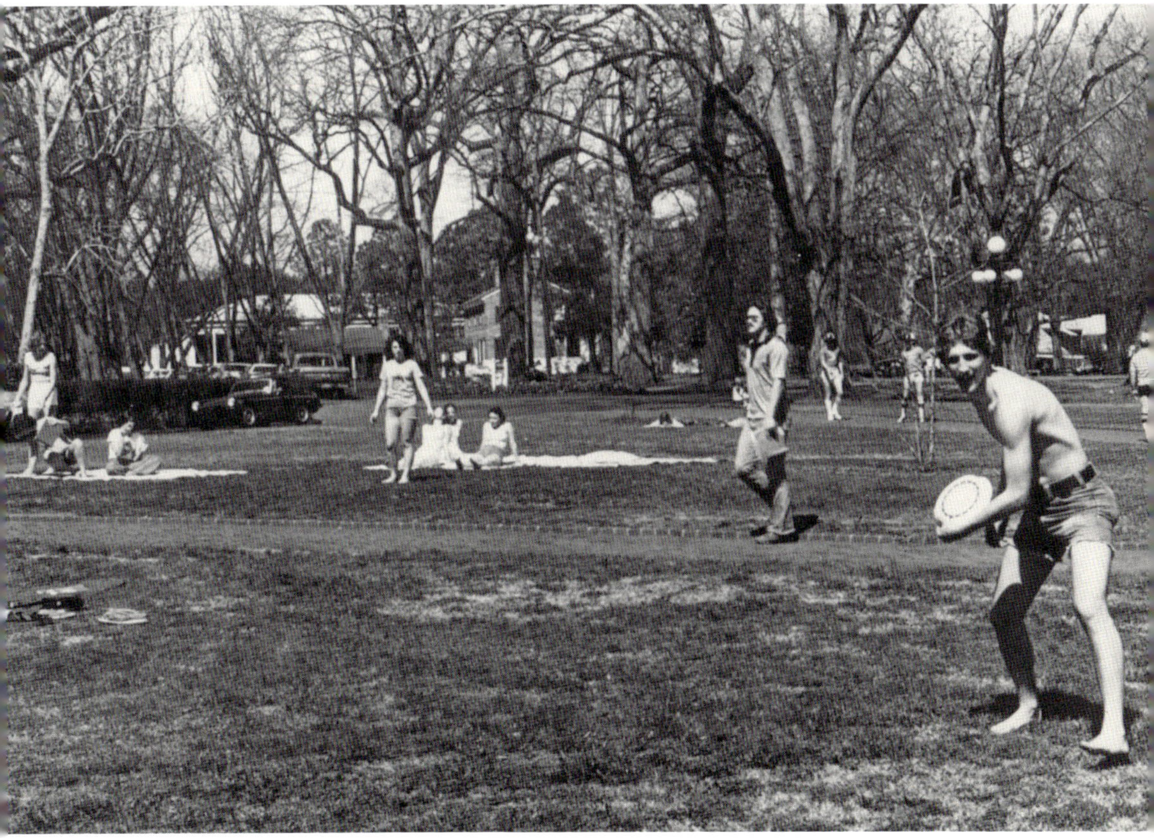

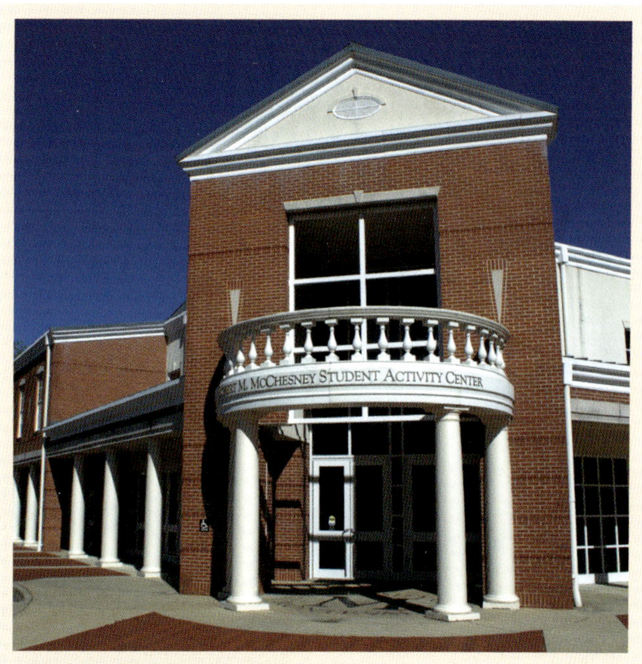

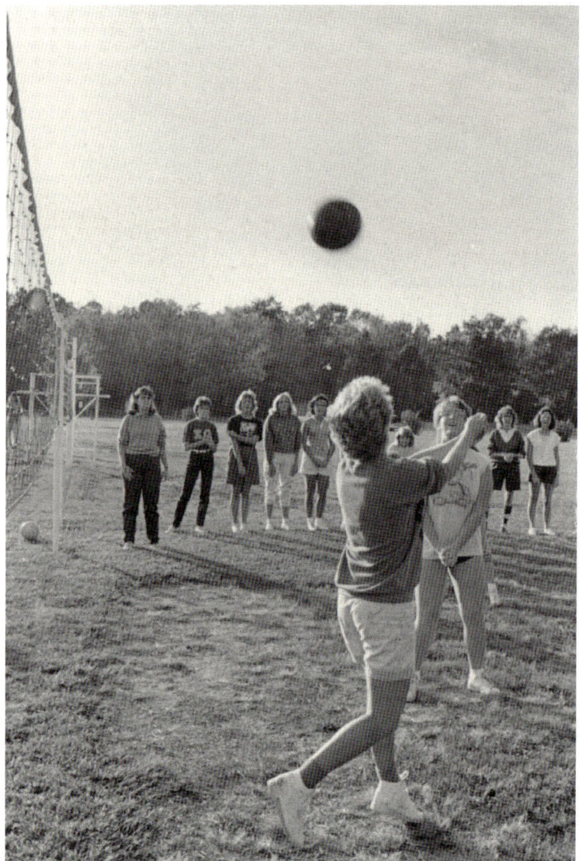

By the late 1990s, the university gymnasium, Myrick Hall, became inadequate for campus needs. In 2004, the university inaugurated the 90,000-square-foot Student Activity Center, the "SAC," later named for 13th president Robert M. McChesney. It features a natatorium, a 3,000-seat arena, a weight room, a walking track, the Partidge Hall of Fame, and offices for university athletics. The building hosts December commencement and campus recruiting events. The SAC occupies a cluster of former intramural fields seen here.

CHAPTER 3

Town and Points of Interest

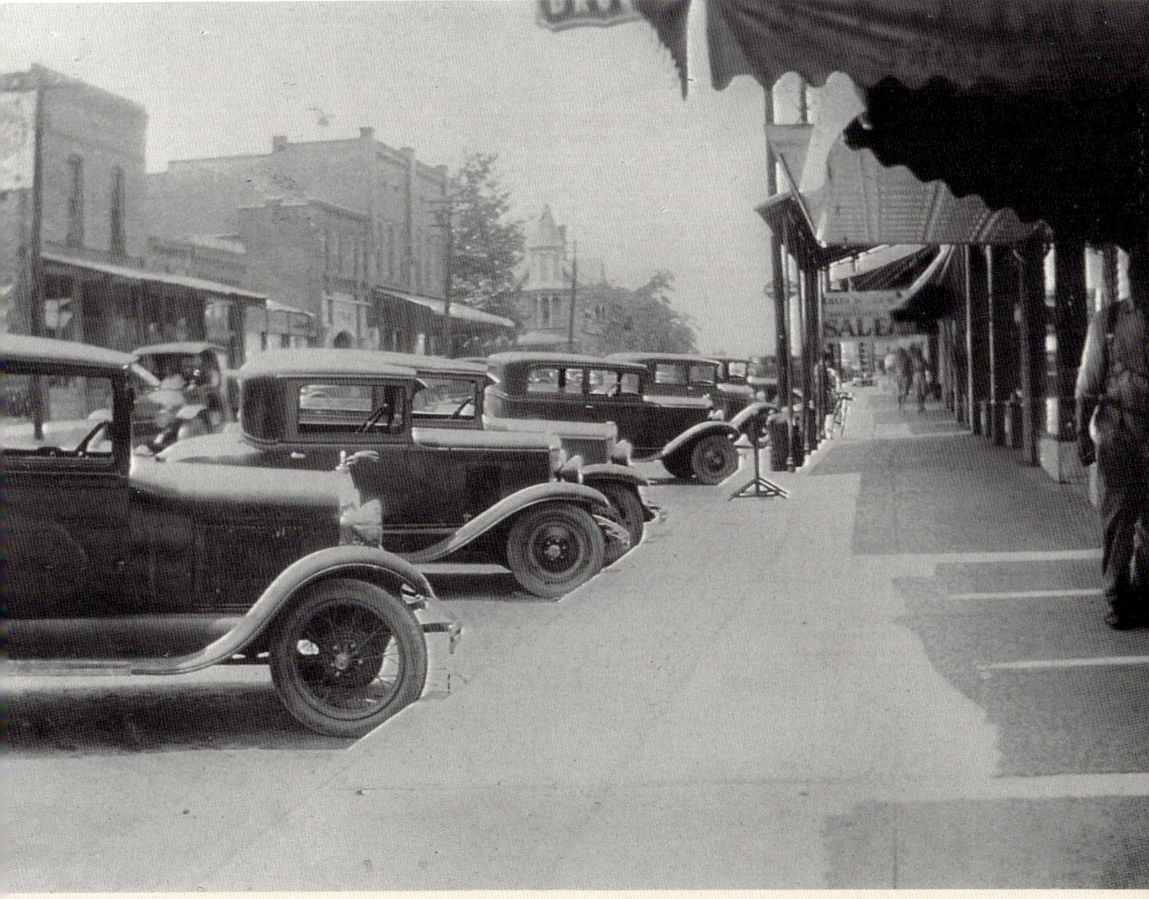

Montevallo benefited in the 1920s from the Good Roads Movement of the previous decade, which witnessed the paving of roads throughout the state. This c. 1930 image shows parked cars in front of a generous sidewalk along Main Street with various retailers. In the center sits the now-demolished Magnolia Hotel. The "sale" sign is for E. Baer Dry Goods.

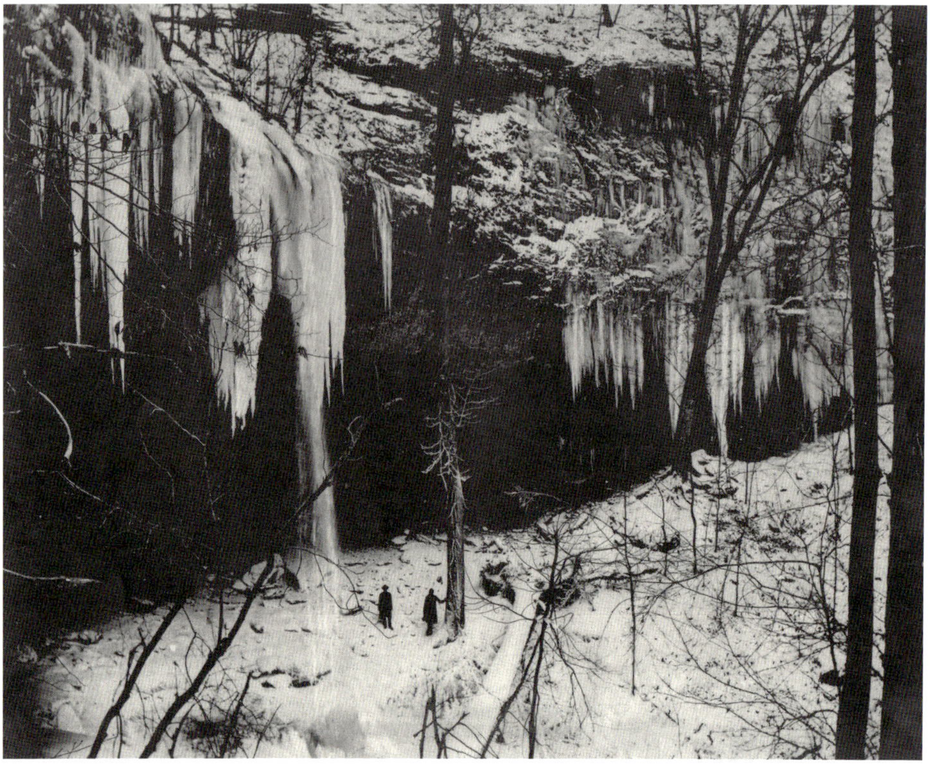

The Cahaba River National Wildlife Refuge, six miles from Montevallo, has a 90-foot waterfall, Falling Rock, overlooking a small natural cavern. The falls, seen here in about 1900, are off the main road, and visitors need to be aware of the slippery watercourse above the falls. Students in the 1920s had "picnic parties" at the site, chaperoned by a faculty member. Today, the university's Environmental Studies provides biannual clean-ups to rid the area of trash and accumulated debris.

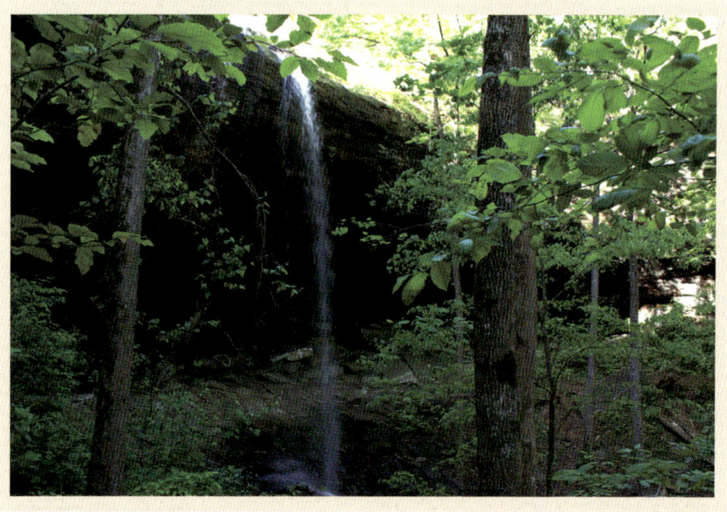

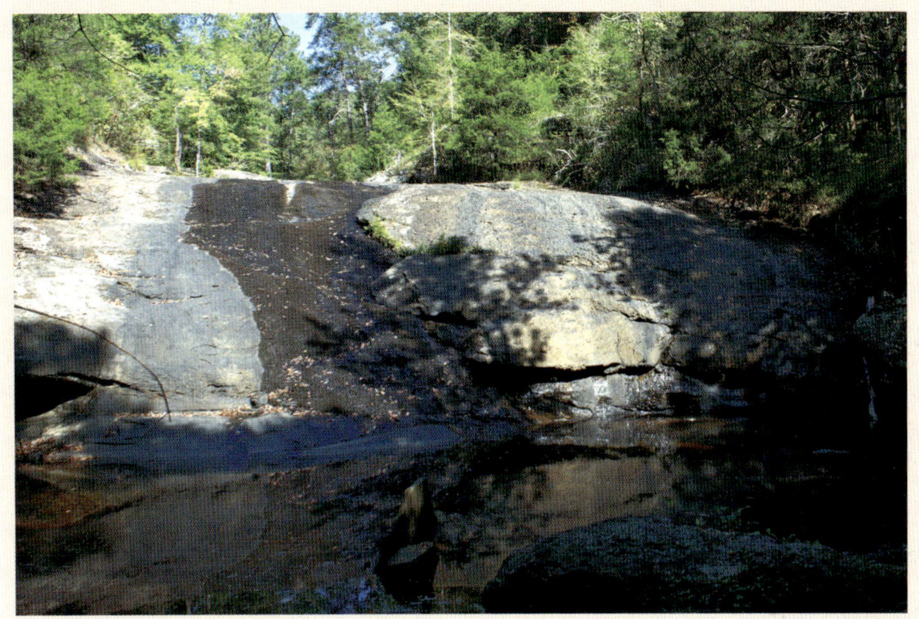

Located two miles from downtown Montevallo and named after one of the early settling families, Davis Creek and Falls was a place of recreation and refuge for those who lived in town or attended the college, as seen in this c. 1900 photograph. A series of small cascades accompanied by stone picnic tables on the upper bank, the locale provided natural air-conditioning during warmer months. Today, timber and logging concerns own the area around the falls.

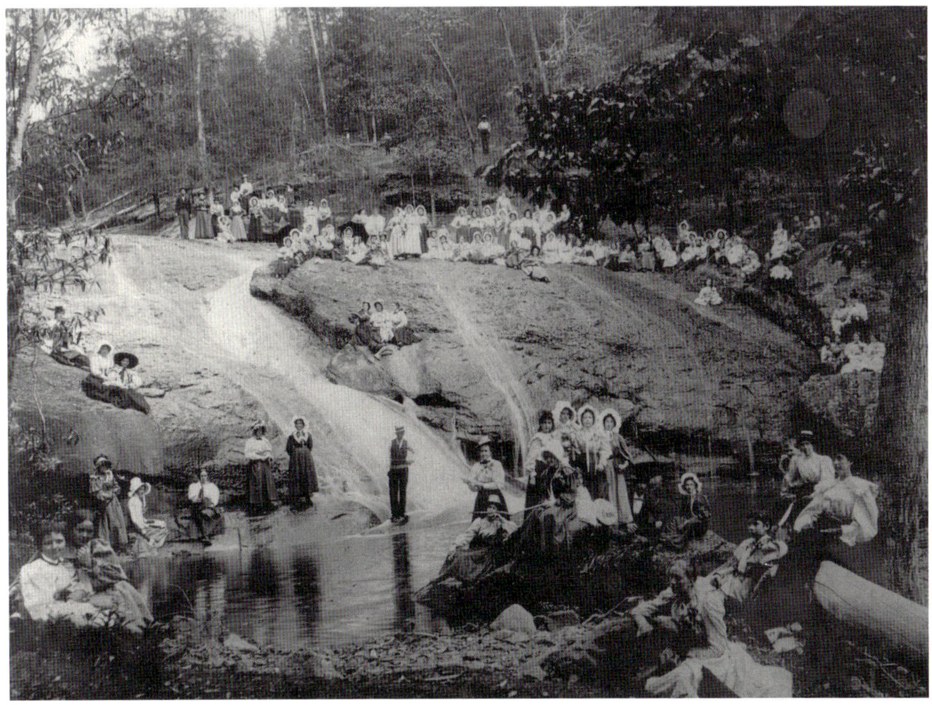

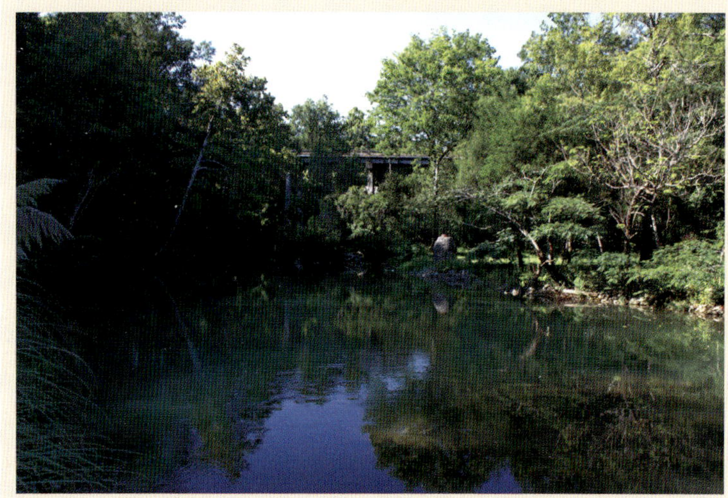

This c. 1900 photograph shows a young boy and cows in Shoal Creek. The creek, which meanders through town, was a source of drinking water for both residents and livestock. The college pumped water from Big Springs in Shoal Creek to two campus water towers so that students and residents would have pressurized water. Shoal Creek was also the source of severe flooding until the 1960s, when the current Orr Park was built to ease this problem.

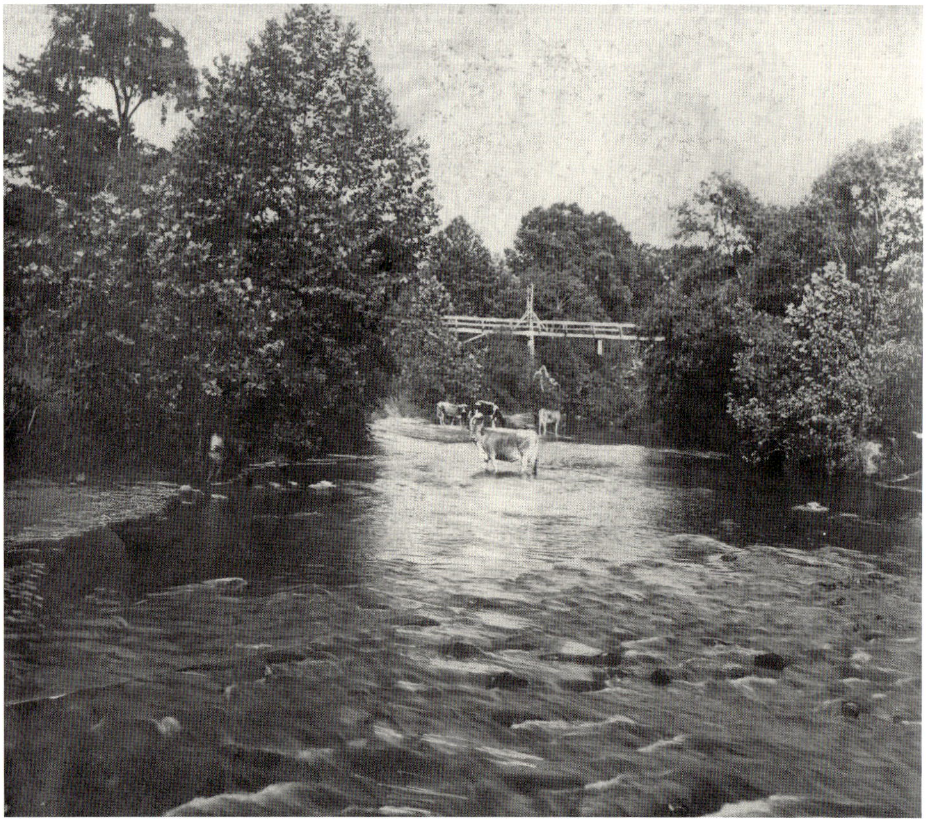

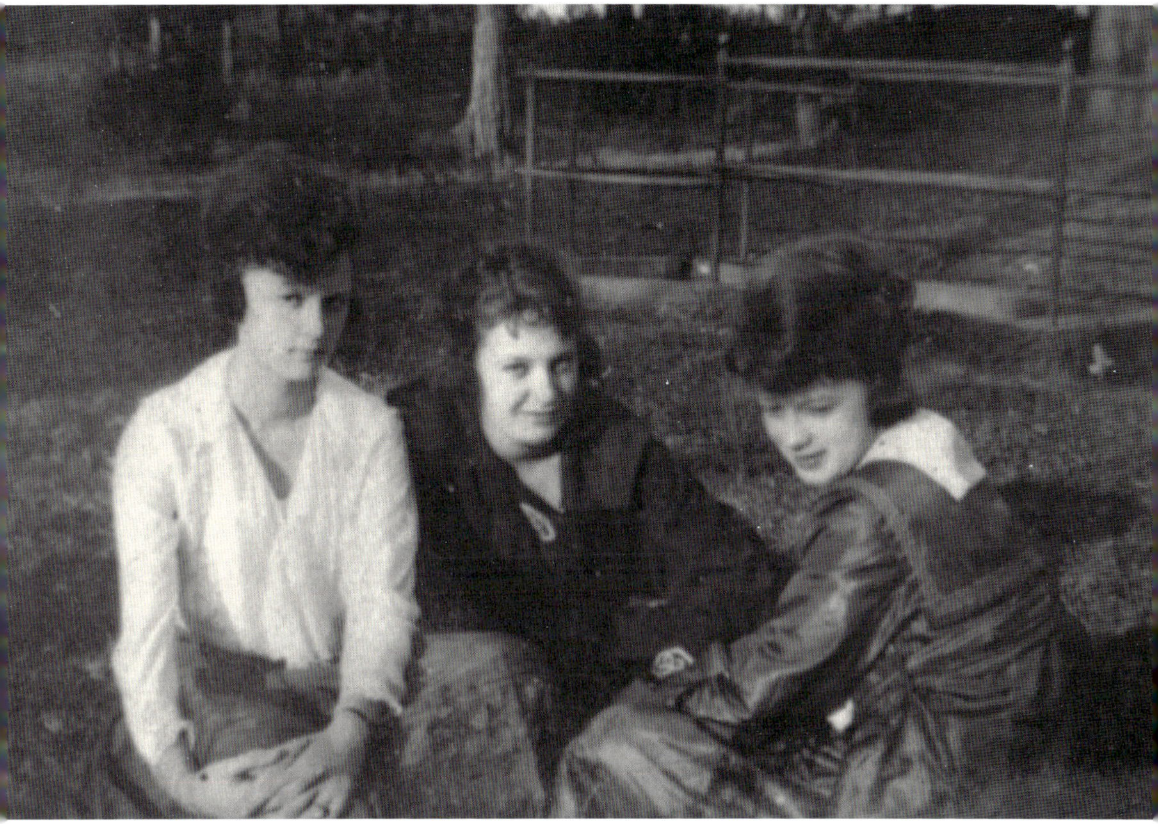

Big Springs, next to Shoal Creek near the section nicknamed "Frog Holler," was a source of water for the college. Big Springs also offered local recreation as a place to fish and swim. The town named the area Orr Park in the 1970s and, in 1989, created a limestone and river-rock waterfall on top of the spring. The park is home to several annual events, including the popular Cars by the Creek and Tinglewood Festival, which highlights woodcarving.

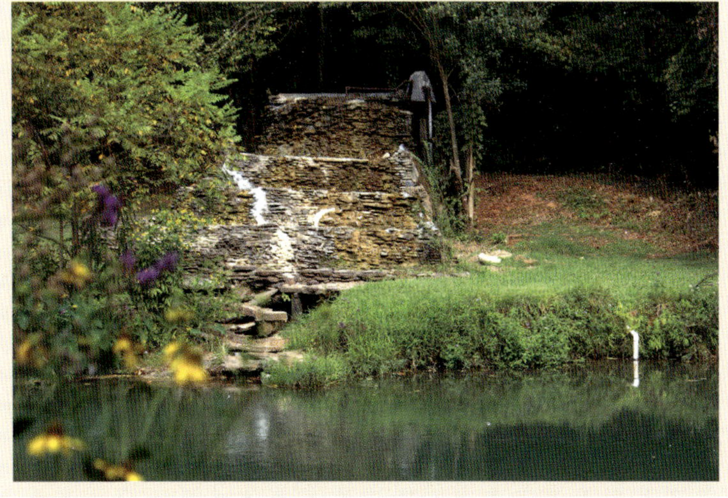

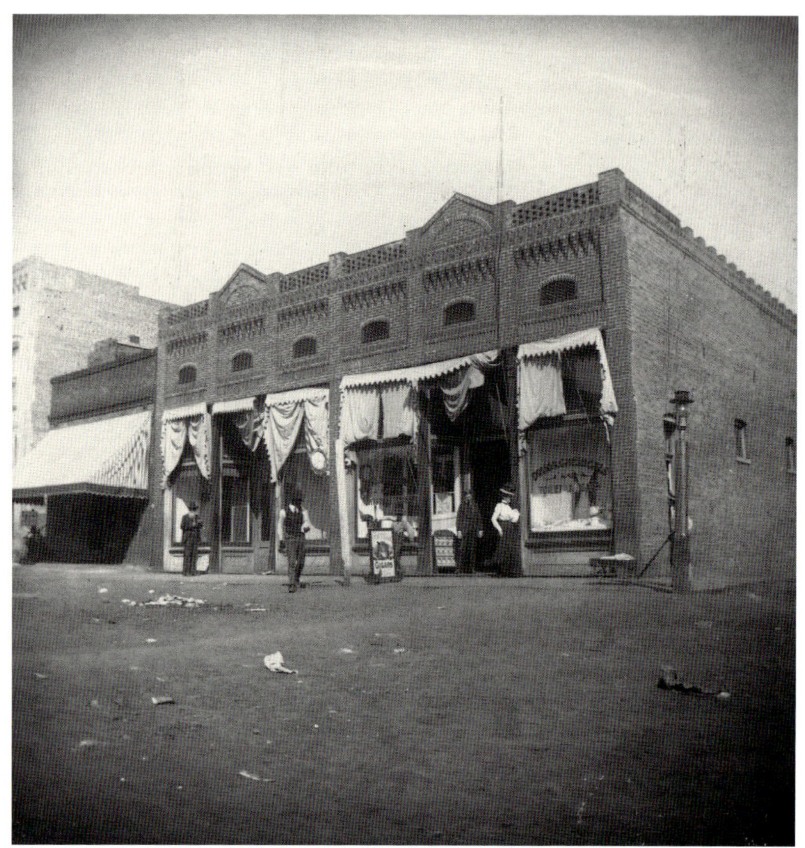

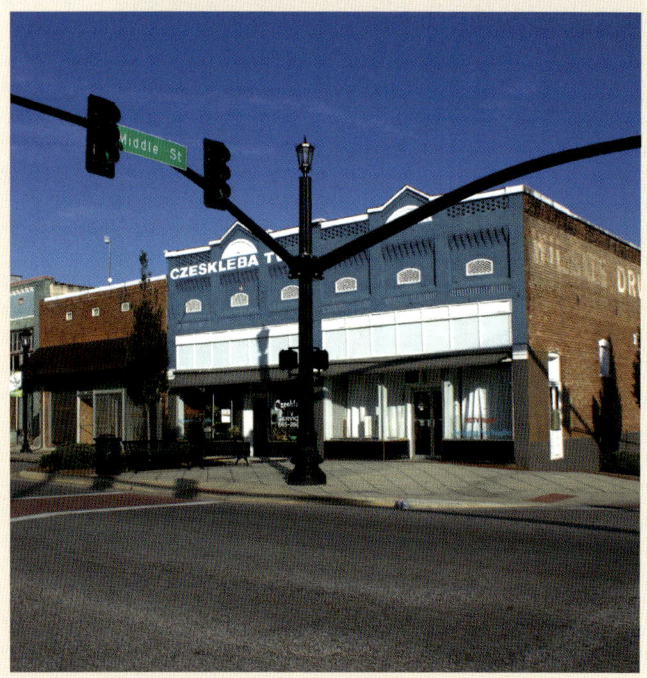

This late-1890s photograph shows one of the oldest structures downtown at Main and Middle Streets. This retailer sold drugs, art supplies, toilet articles, and cigars. Since then, the building has housed a variety of retailers over the years. Ben Franklin and Wilson Drugs (and later Wilson Sundries) were longtime tenants, as was McClure Drug. Walt Czeskleba's Czeskleba TV Service store has been in business since 1972 and at this particular site since 1975.

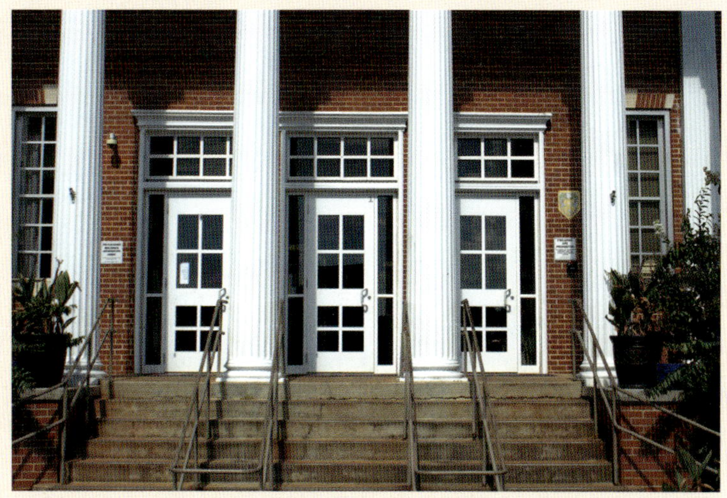

Secondary education in Montevallo found itself in different sites up to the early 1900s. By 1924, Alabama College established a Laboratory Training School in Reynolds Hall that operated until 1930. The city built Montevallo High School in a handsome Greek Revival style in 1930; it had nine classrooms as enrollment increased to over 400 students. Works Progress Administration funding in 1940 added two more wings. This c. 1953 photograph shows the Montevallo High School Band.

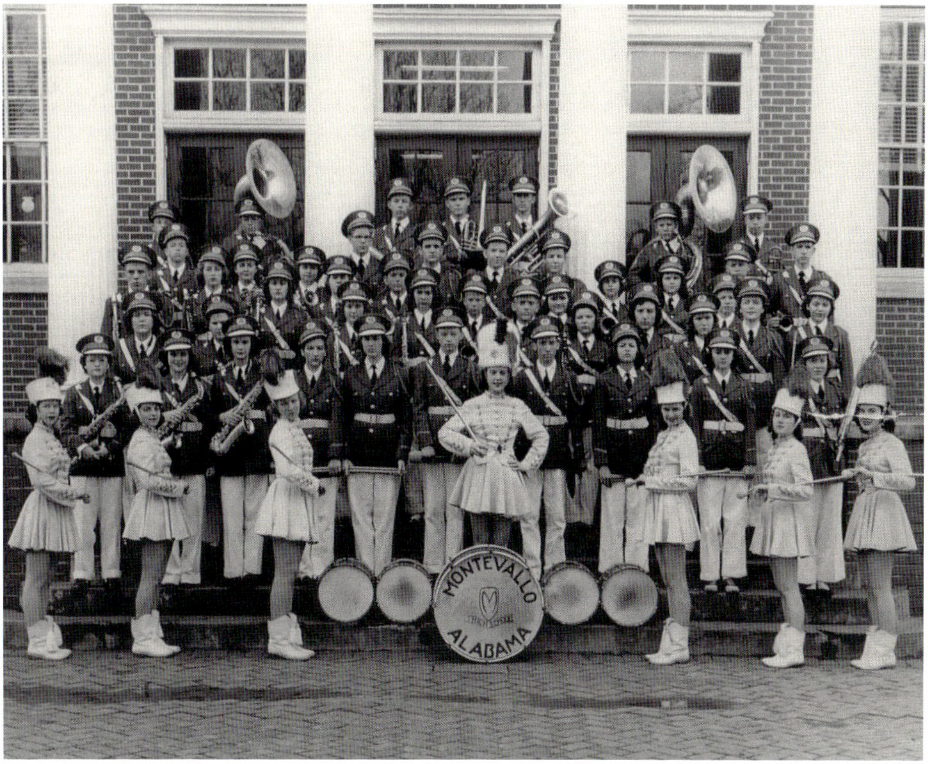

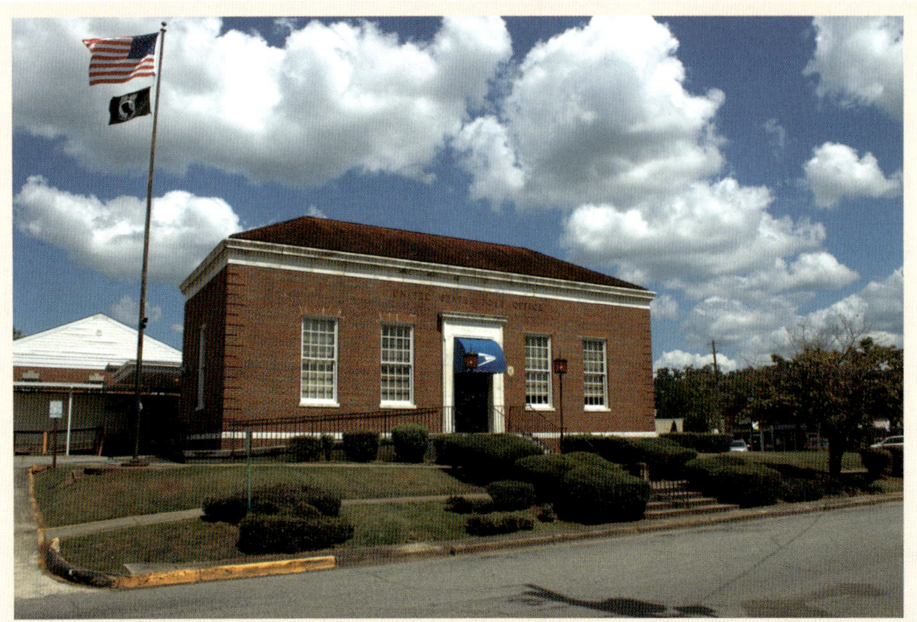

The city has received regular mail service since 1826, when it changed its name to Montevallo from Wilson's Hill, as another post office bore that name. This first post office was on Main Street. With the need for a newer structure, Public Works Administration funding of $52,000 allowed the Montevallo Post Office to move to its current, spacious location on Vine Street in 1937. The interior features vaulted ceilings, Georgian marble decor, a red slate roof, and a large agricultural mural.

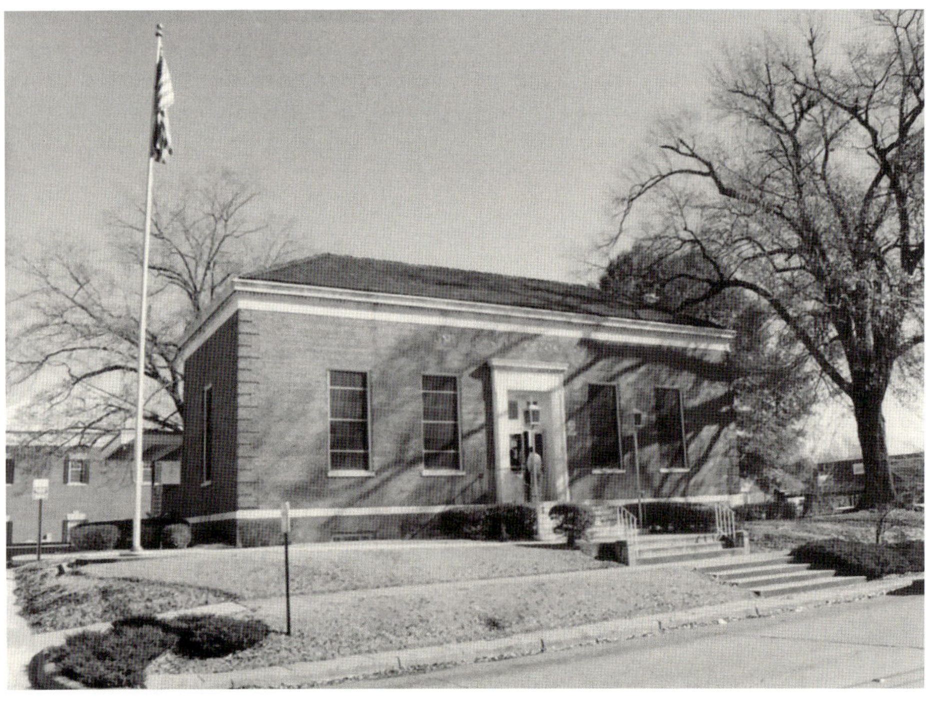

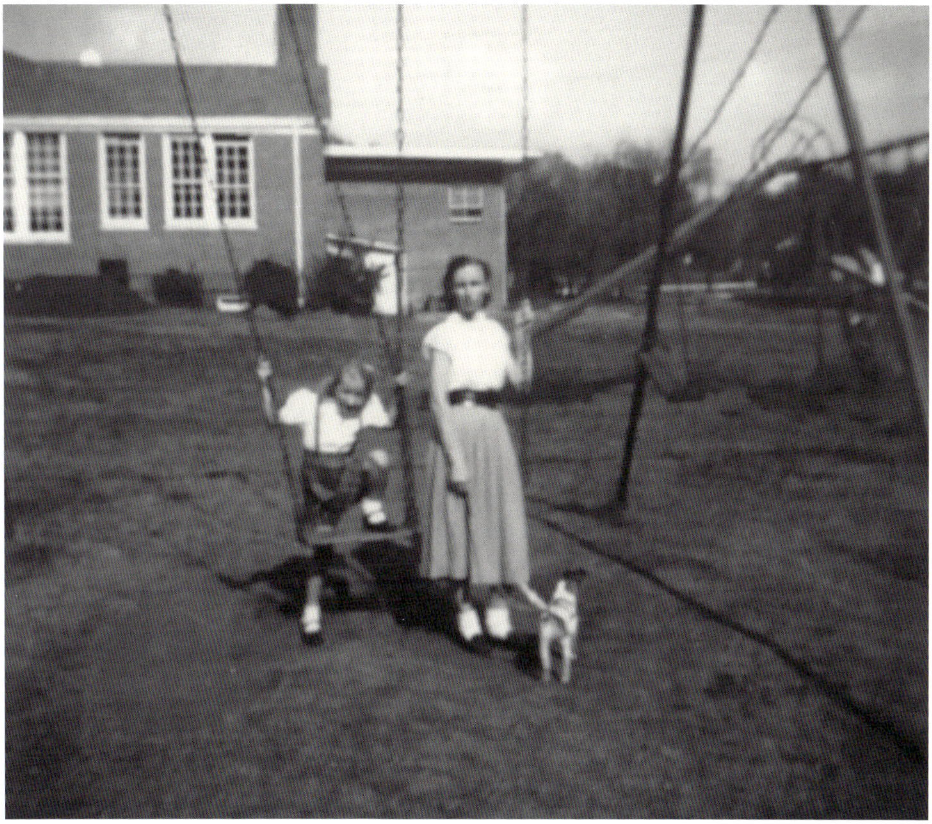

As school enrollment continued to increase, the city built the Alice Boyd Building in 1939 next to the high school. Also in a Greek Revival style, the building added four classrooms and two activity rooms. Alice Boyd, with degrees from Peabody College and Columbia University, had been a faculty member at Alabama College for 13 years before becoming principal of Montevallo Elementary School. She passed away in 1936, and the school named this new structure after her.

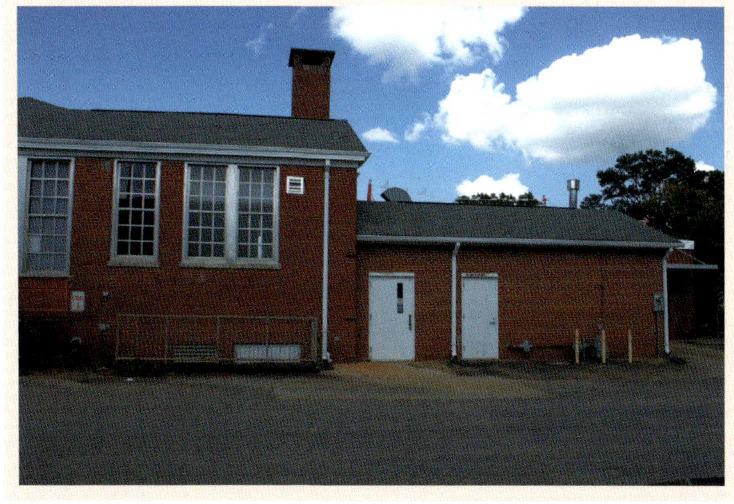

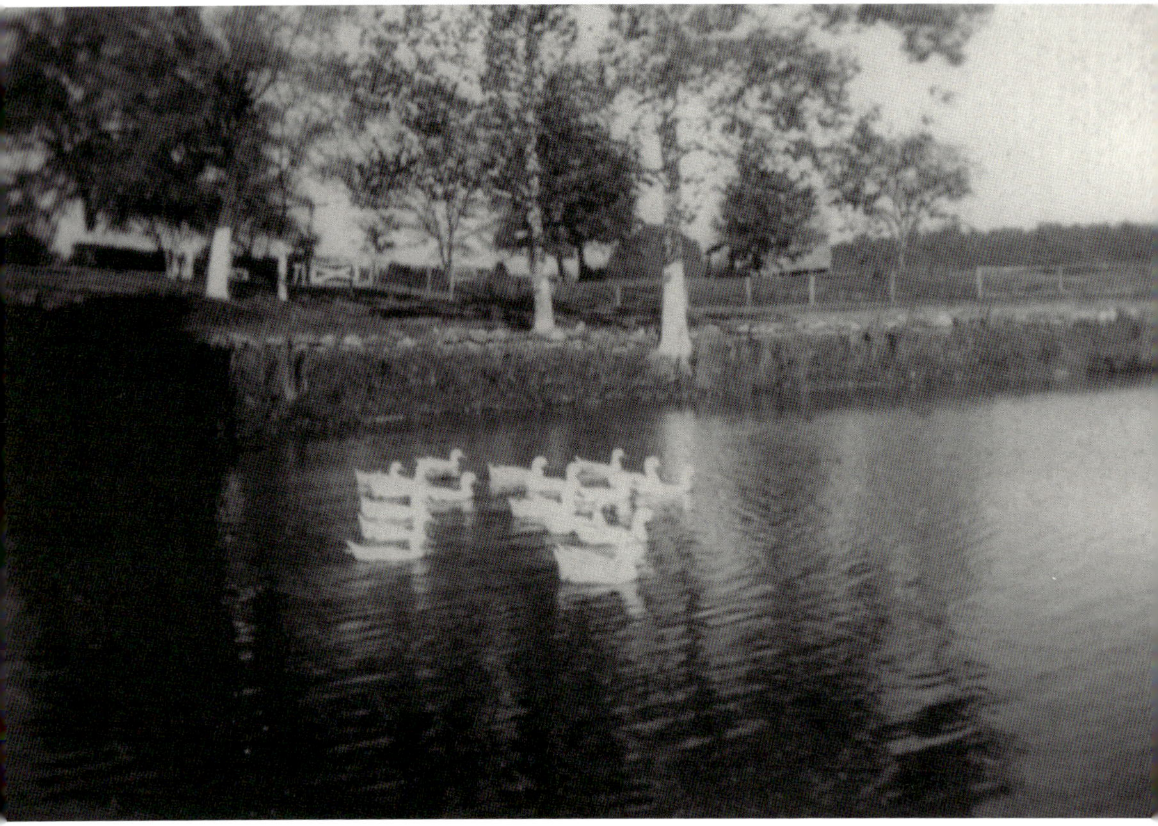

Ebenezer, a small settlement just north of town, features a pristine lowland swamp. The spring-fed area hosts a rare species of plant and several important limestone aquifers underground. The university conducts field trips and classes in environmental education for both university and grade-school students and features an extensive boardwalk for traversing the preserve. The vintage image shows Bolton Farm Lake, which was fed from a large Ebenezer Swamp spring on Arthur Bolton's farm. (Past image courtesy of Becky Bolton.)

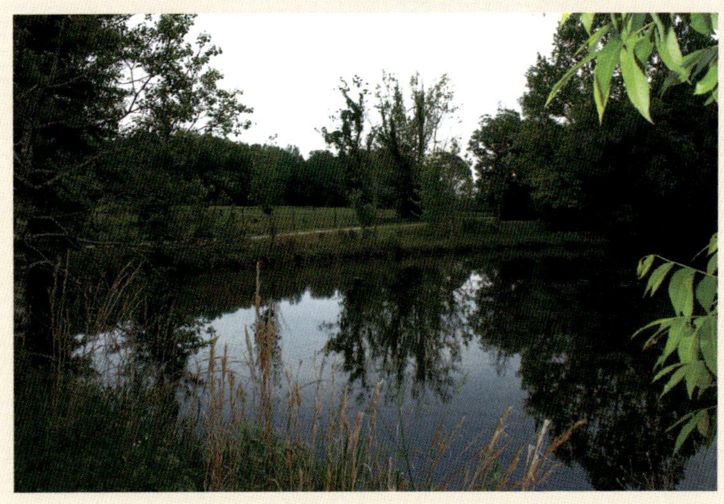

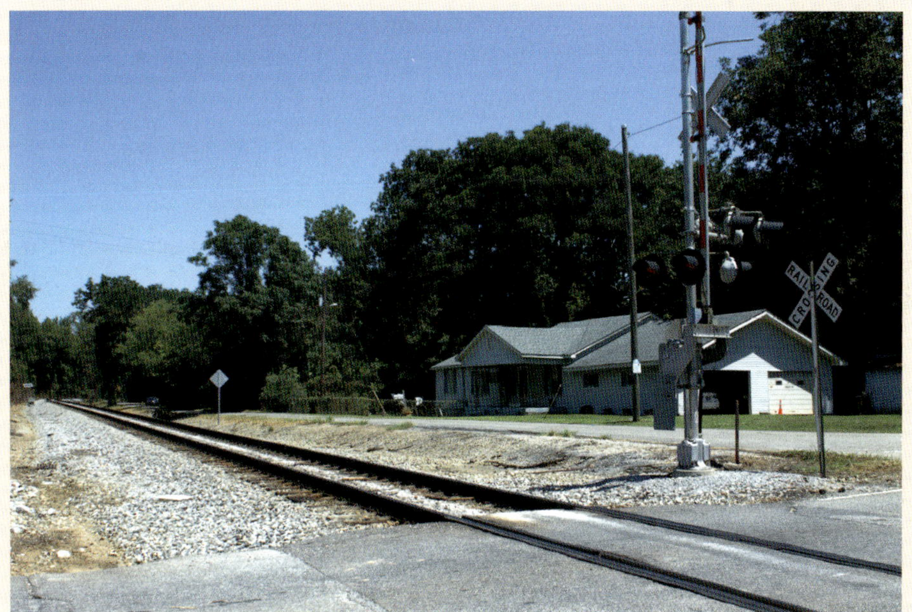

Coal mining had been a major employer in the Montevallo region starting in the 1850s. After World War II, mining declined, and increasingly the timber industry became important. This Mahler logging truck photograph from 1947 was taken in the satellite town of Aldrich, just a couple of miles from downtown Montevallo. Today, it is not uncommon to see logging trucks pass through downtown on their way to timber processing facilities.

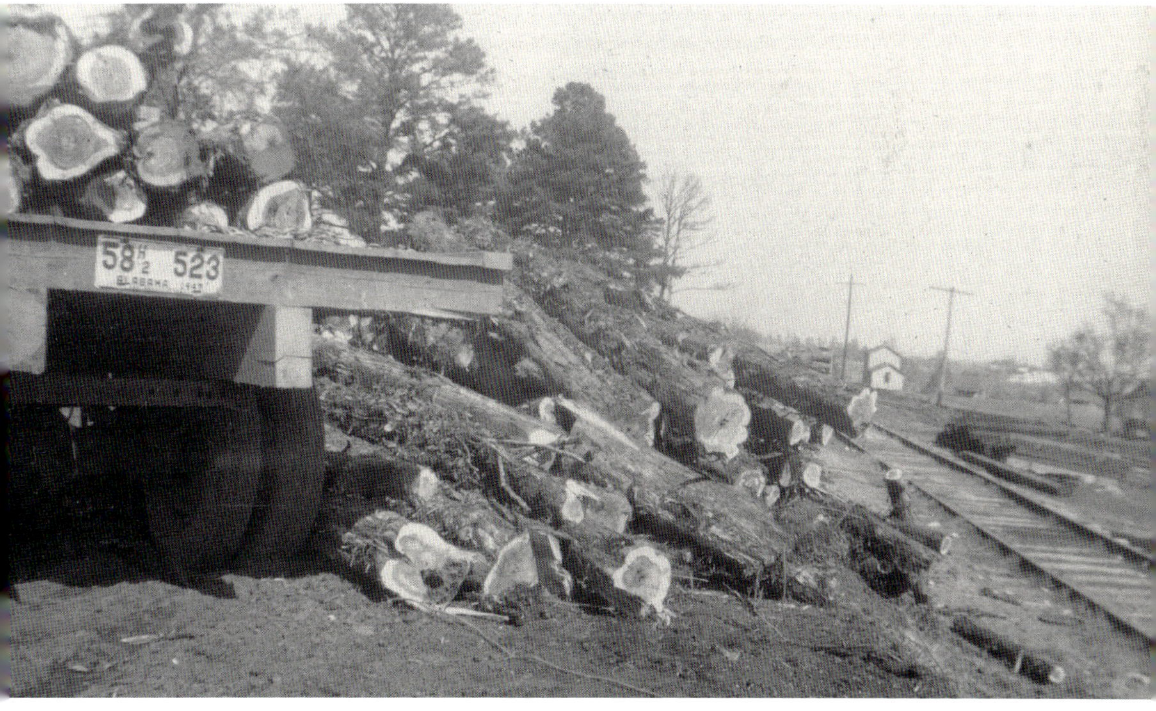

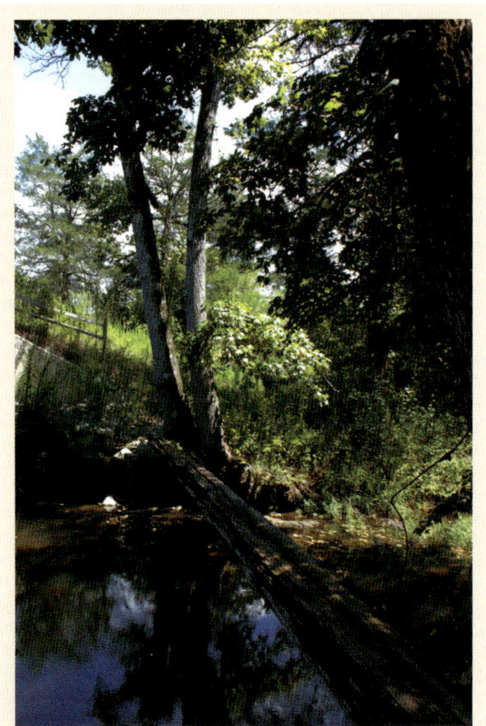

In 1946, the Mahler family purchased the home and remaining land that once belonged to antebellum planter Jacob Perry. Betty Mahler donated the farm to the city in 2013. Shoal Creek Park currently features the home, a cemetery related to one of the area's original churches, a pavilion, and 10 miles of hiking trails. This 1955 photograph shows Mahler cousins Joann ? (left) and Carol ? (right) returning from picking berries on an old log footbridge.

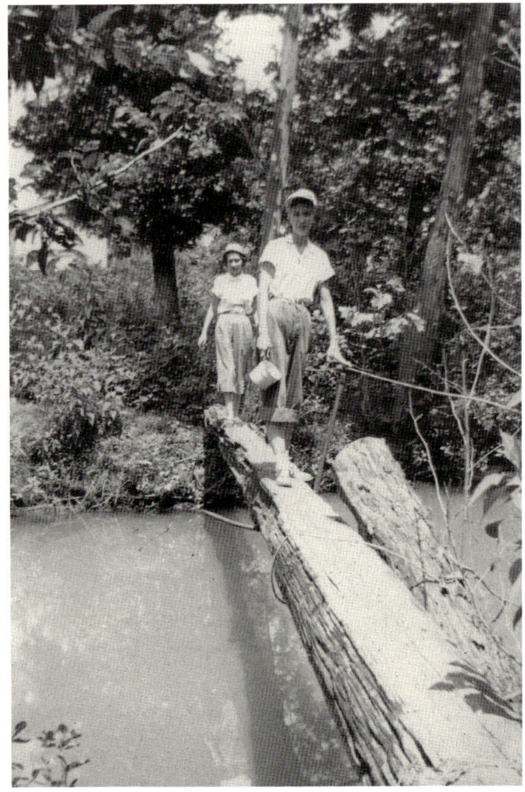

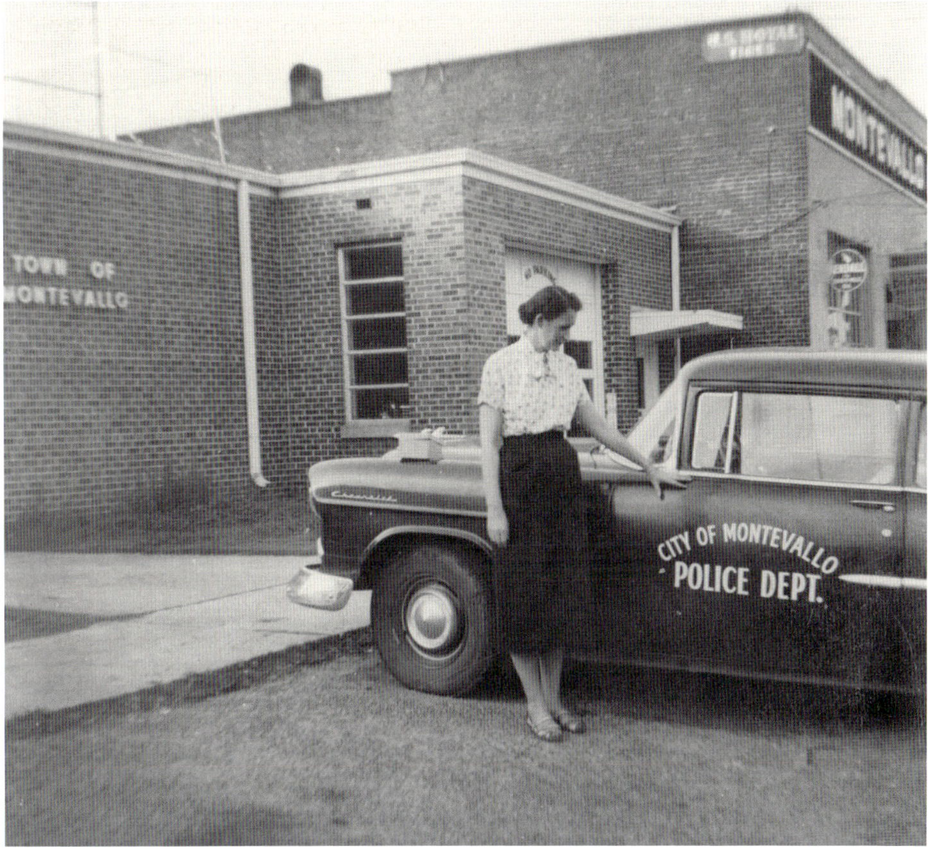

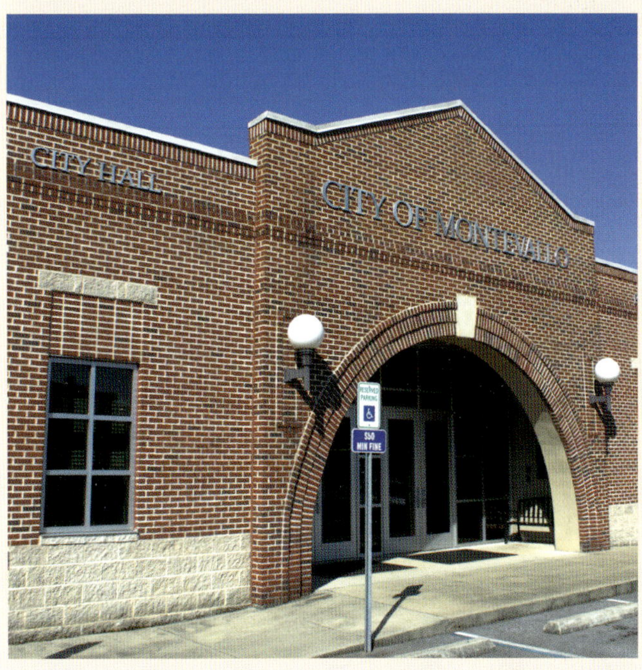

In 1948, the City of Montevallo accepted bids for a city hall as the older structure had outlived its usefulness. This mid-1950s photograph shows the "new" city hall, next to the Victory Auto building. By the early 2000s, the city again needed a more modern space. Ground was broken in 2014, and the new building was completed in 2015. The new structure has over 1,000 more square feet and larger council chambers that can accommodate over 100 visitors.

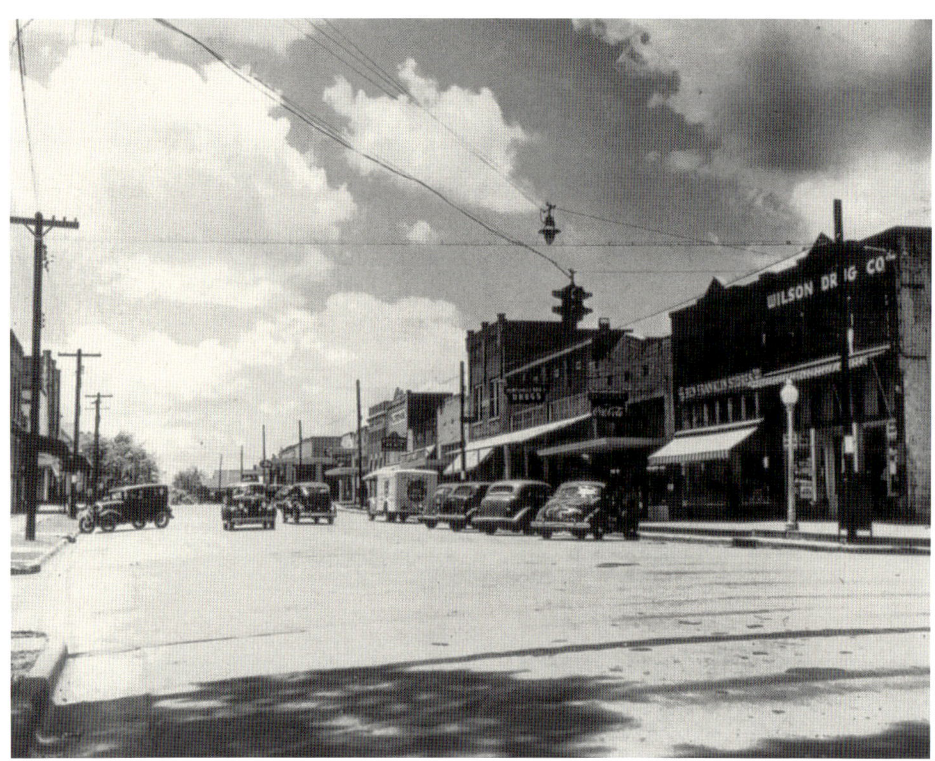

Montevallo's Main Street has been a consistent hub of activity for those who live in town, for those passing through to satellite towns nearby, and for those driving in for the day for business, shopping, or eating. In 2019, Netflix filmed select 1950s location shots here for the period film *The Devil All the Time* with a cast including Tom Holland, Bill Skarsgård, Robert Pattinson, and Mia Wasikowska. A 2014 state grant facilitated an upgrade of downtown sidewalks, traffic lights, and parking.

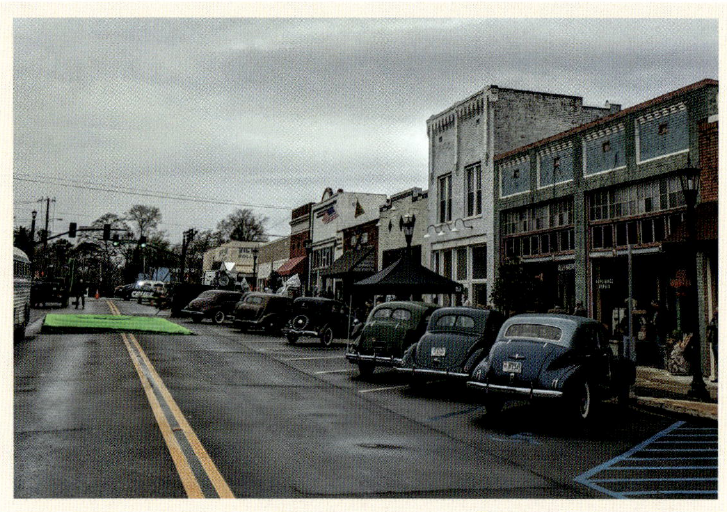

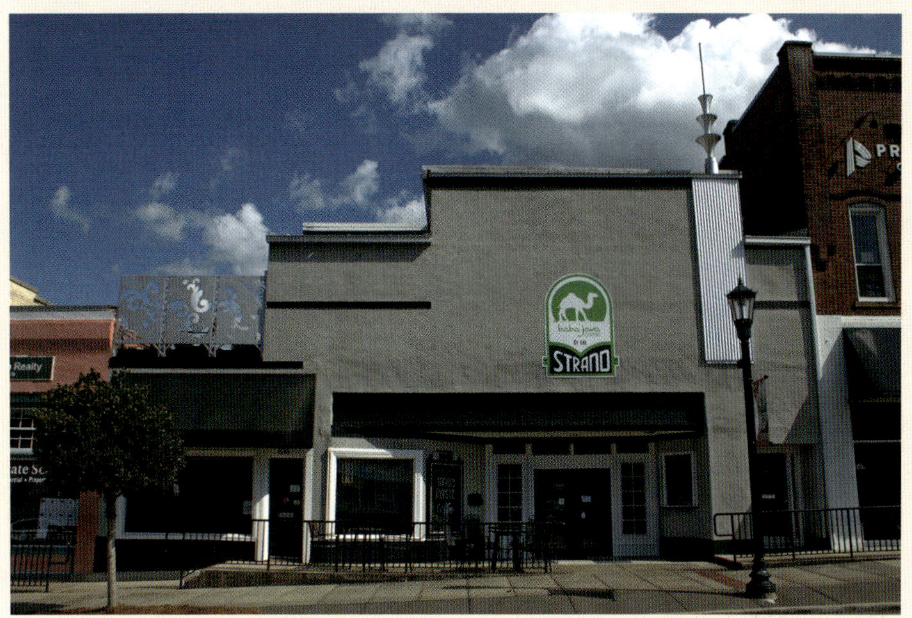

Ruth Watson and her son Eddie opened the Strand Theatre in 1920. In 1935, Eddie Watson built a larger movie house, doubling the capacity with "modern sound and heating systems." The quality of big box office stars is apparent in this 1961 photograph of the marquee. By the 1980s, the theater closed due to competition with larger movie complexes, and the current owner converted it to chic loft apartments and first-floor retail.

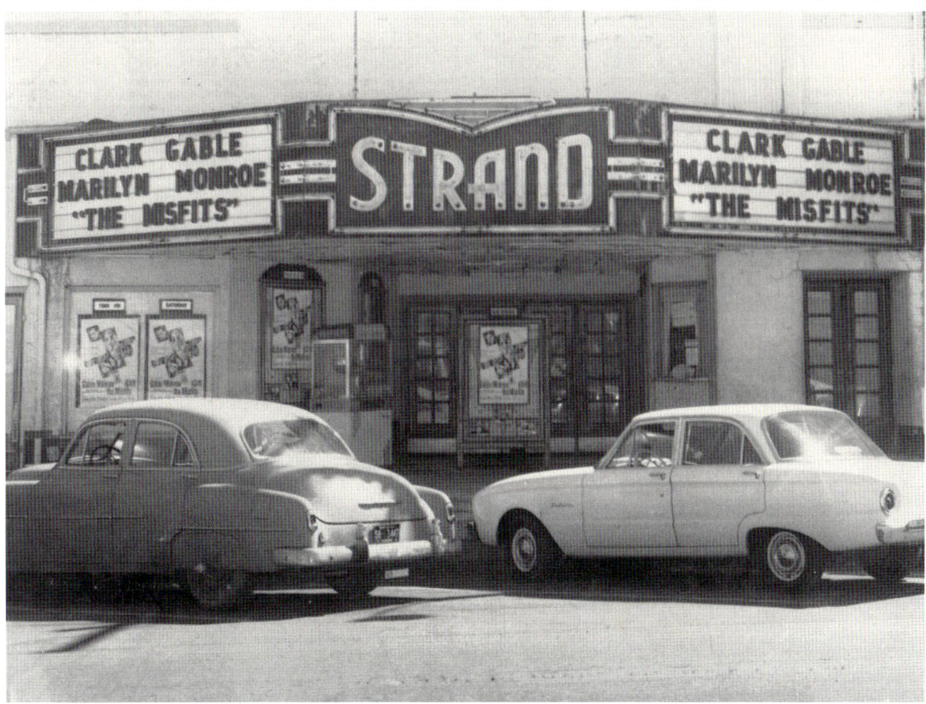

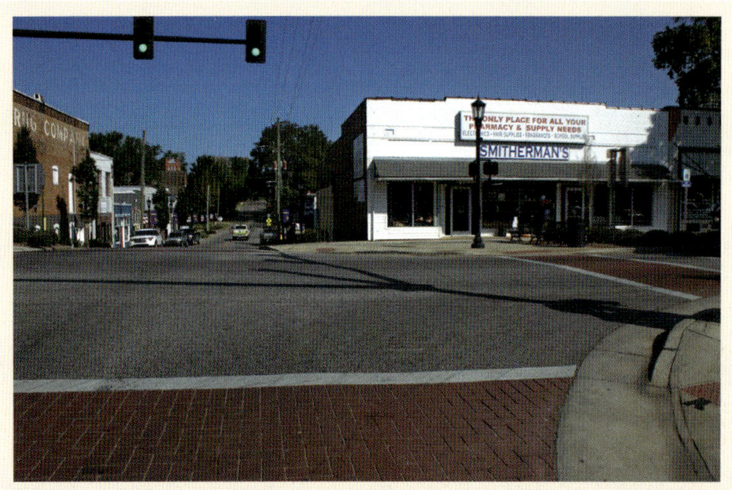

Located on Main Street, from the 1940s, Hicks's Ben Franklin five and dime was a downtown Montevallo institution for over 40 years catering to local residents and college students with a wide variety of products. By the late 1970s, new ownership came, and for nearly a decade, it was Monk's Variety. Today's longtime occupant is Smitherman's Pharmacy, established by pharmacists Larry and Donna Smitherman in the 1980s. It is one of two independent drugstores in the area.

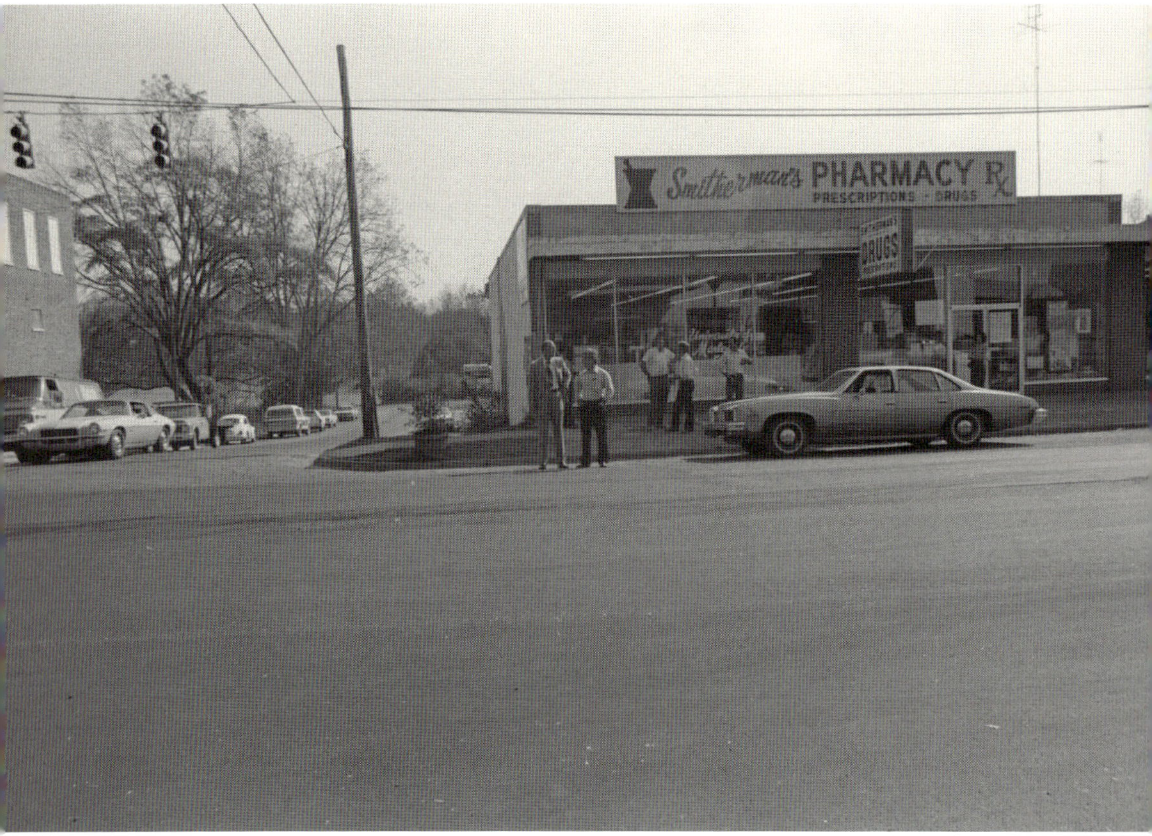

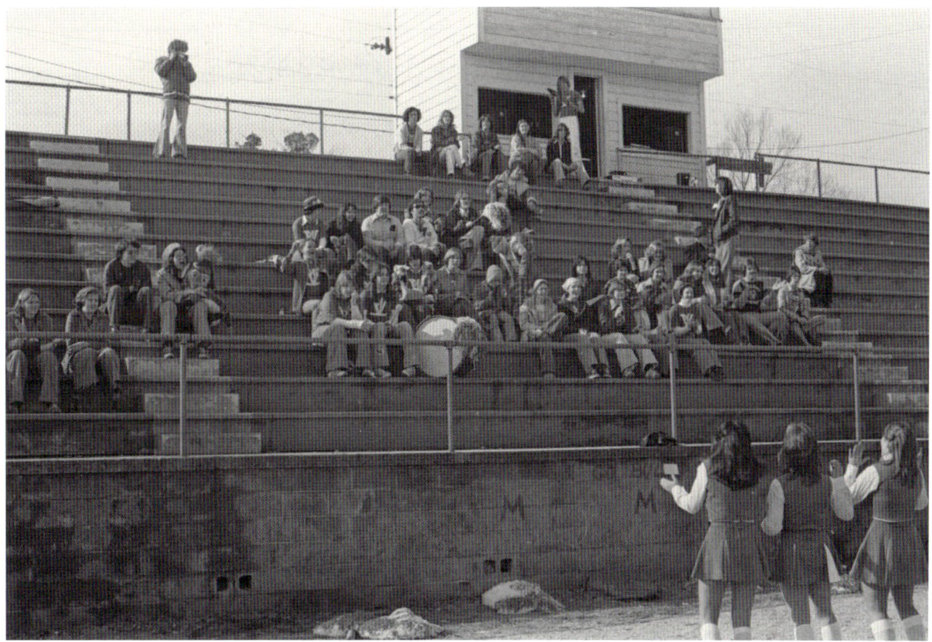

Theron Fisher coached the Montevallo High School Bulldogs football team from 1947 to 1966 and is still the city's longest-tenured coach. Richard Gilliam became head coach in 1973 and led the integration of the team. In 2006, the city renamed the site the Richard Gilliam Field at Theron Fisher Stadium. This 1977 image shows the stadium and press box. In 2014, the city upgraded the facilities with a larger press box, a windscreen, and a resurfacing of the track.

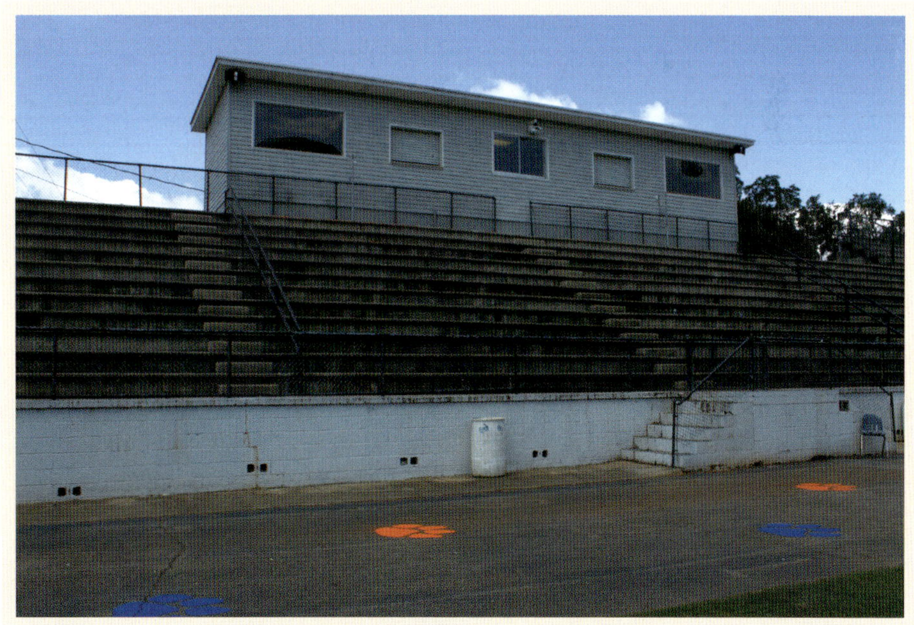

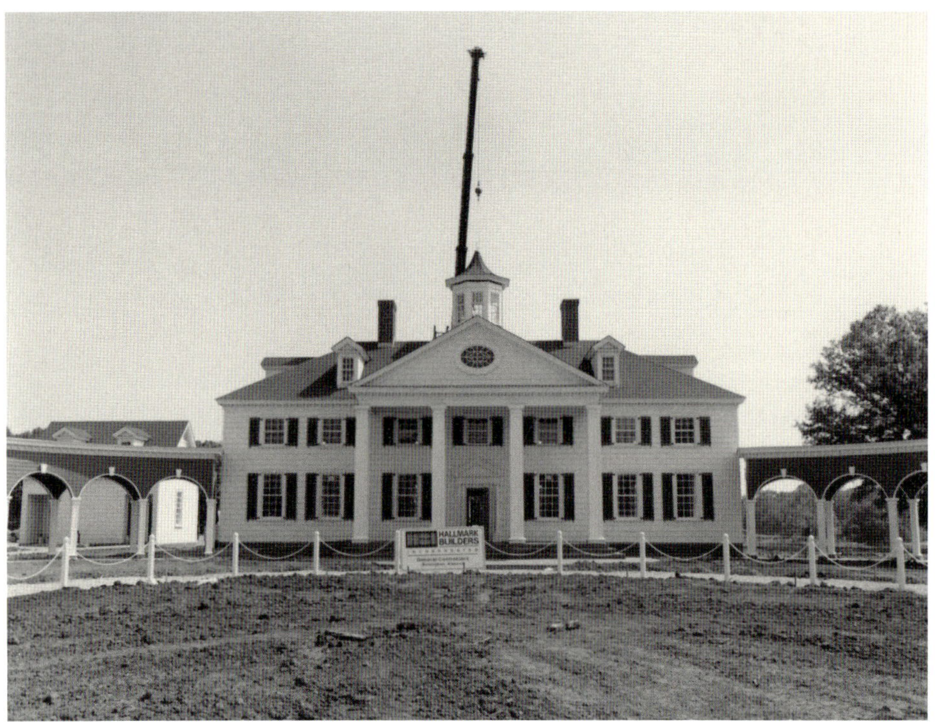

The American Village, conceived in the late 1980s by Thomas "Tom" Walker (currently president emeritus), has pioneered civic education in the state of Alabama through immersive and engaging experiences. The current 188-acre campus includes replicas of Mount Vernon (seen here), a Colonial courthouse, the president's Oval Office and East Room of the White House, Bruton Parish Church of Williamsburg, Concord Bridge, and the Liberty Bell. Several hundred thousand schoolchildren have visited the American Village since its founding in the mid-1990s.

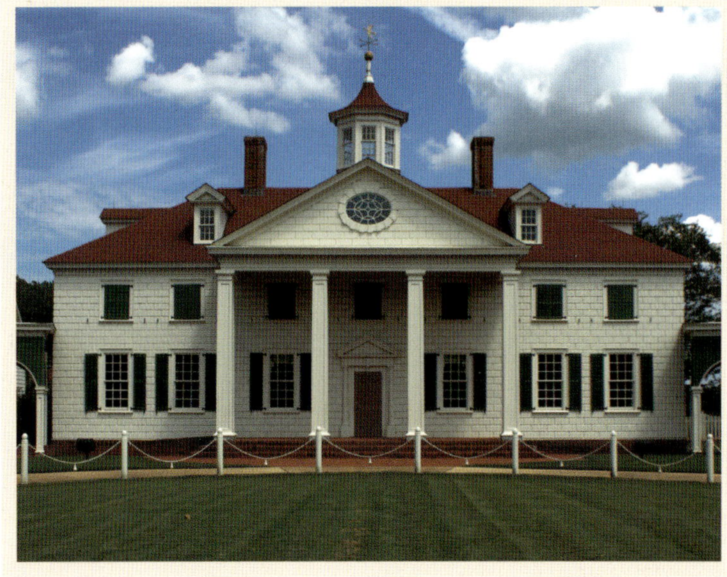

CHAPTER 4

Homes and Churches

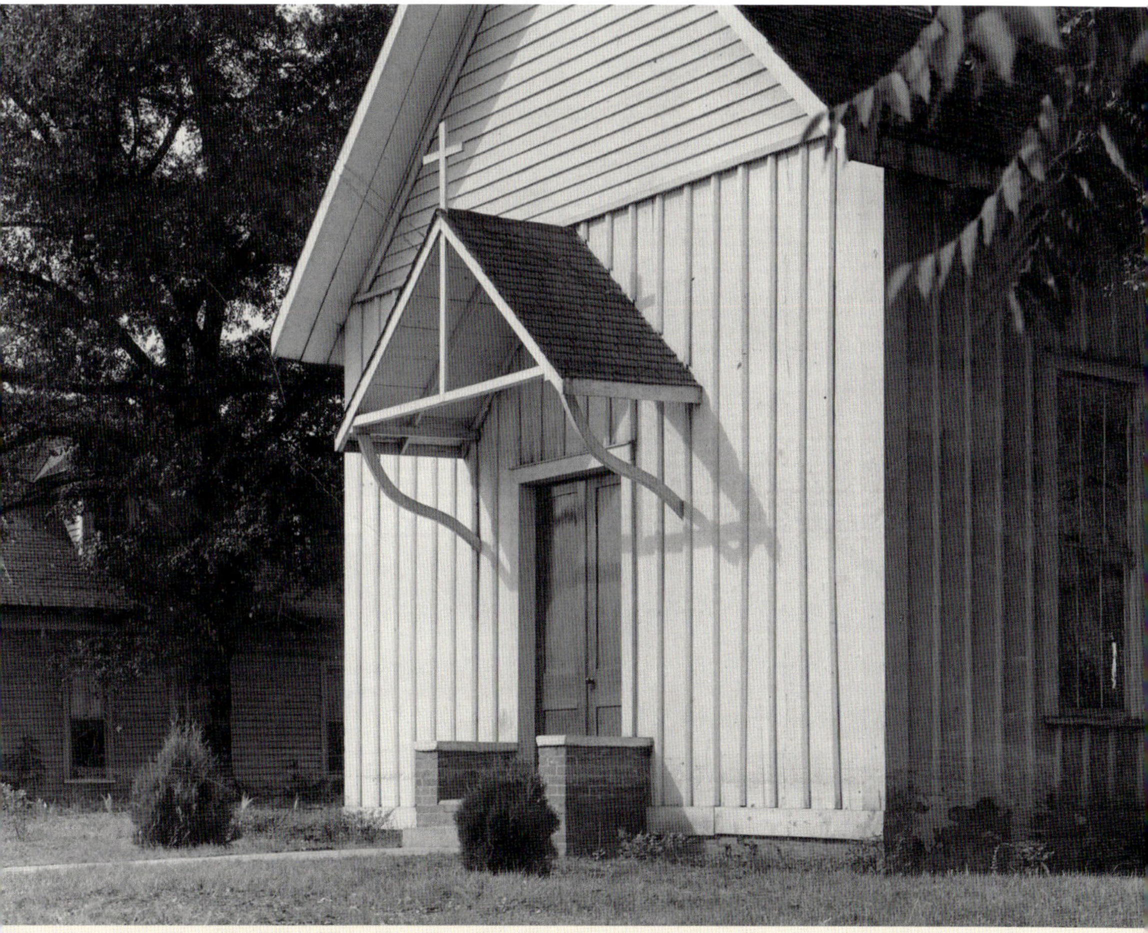

St. Andrew's Episcopal Church first organized and gathered in member homes or public spaces such as the Masonic lodge. In 1860, a priest conducted services on a rotating basis until a proper church was constructed. Both 1873 and 1939 saw tragedy, as storms destroyed the church. St. Andrew's moved to the corner of Plowman and Oak Streets in 1953.

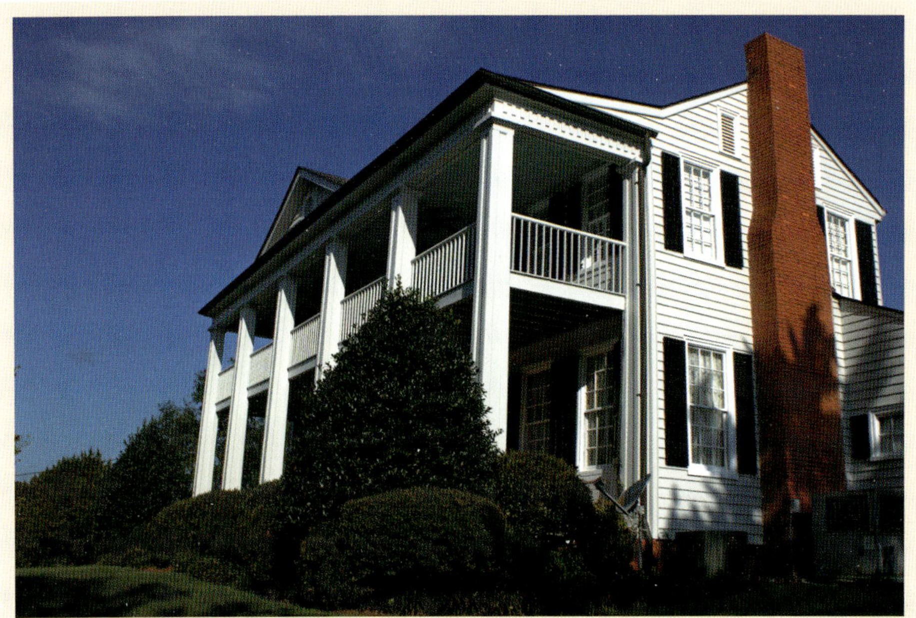

The Cunningham-Stamps home is one of the oldest extant homes in the area. Joseph Cunningham, originally from Virginia, settled in the area and completed the house in the mid-1820s. By the 1850s, the Cunningham plantation covered 800 acres and included 30 enslaved people. The plantation fell into disrepair and sold off plots of land over the years. Sherwood Stamps bought the house in 1963 and restored it to its original charm, adding period-piece furniture throughout.

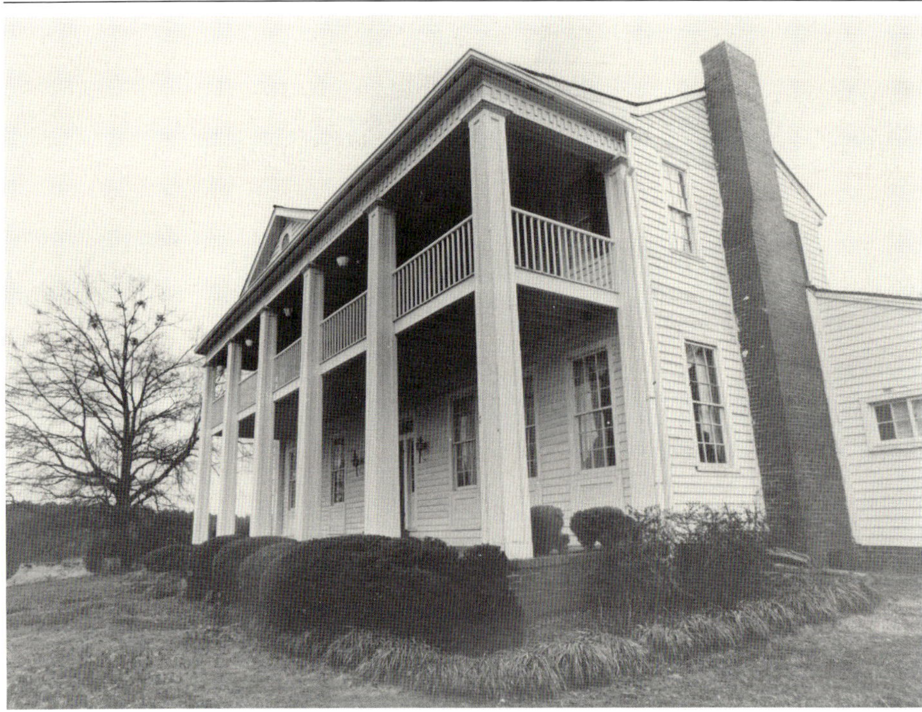

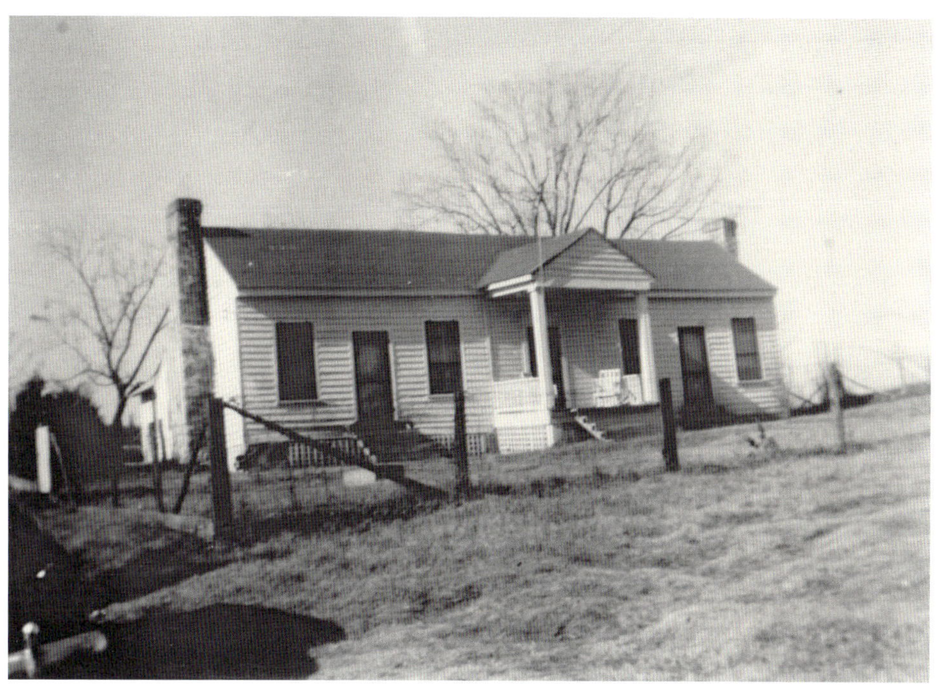

The McGaughy Farm on Salem Road is recognized as an Alabama Century and Heritage Farm. Originally owned by Jacob Perry, the farm was deeded to Washington and Nancy McGaughy around 1836 when the Perrys acquired the nearby plantation now known as Shoal Creek Park. Washington McGaughy served as the Perry overseer through the Civil War years and later farmed the property until his death. Fifth-generation owners Herbert "H.G." Galloway and Doris McGaughy donated the farmstead to the University of Montevallo.

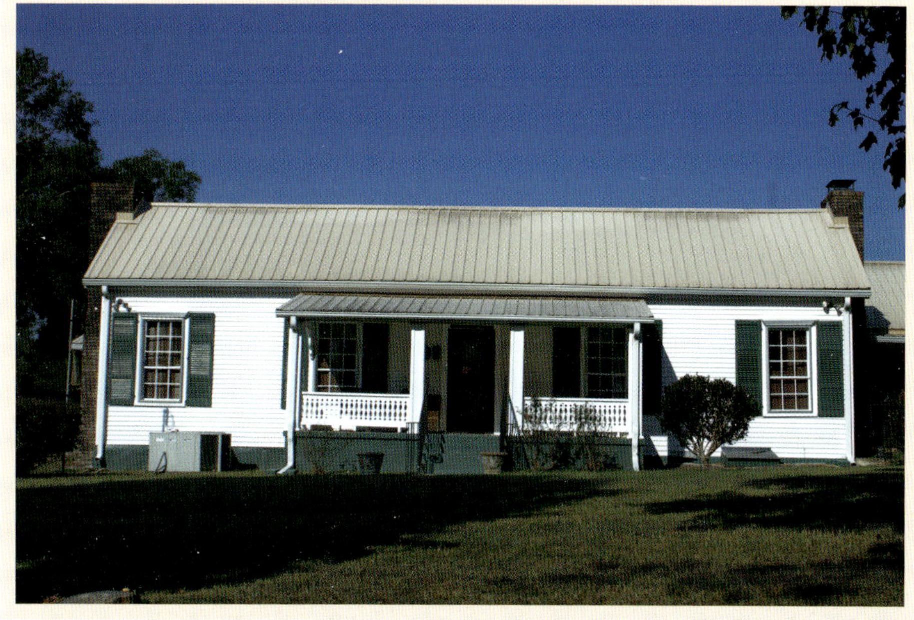

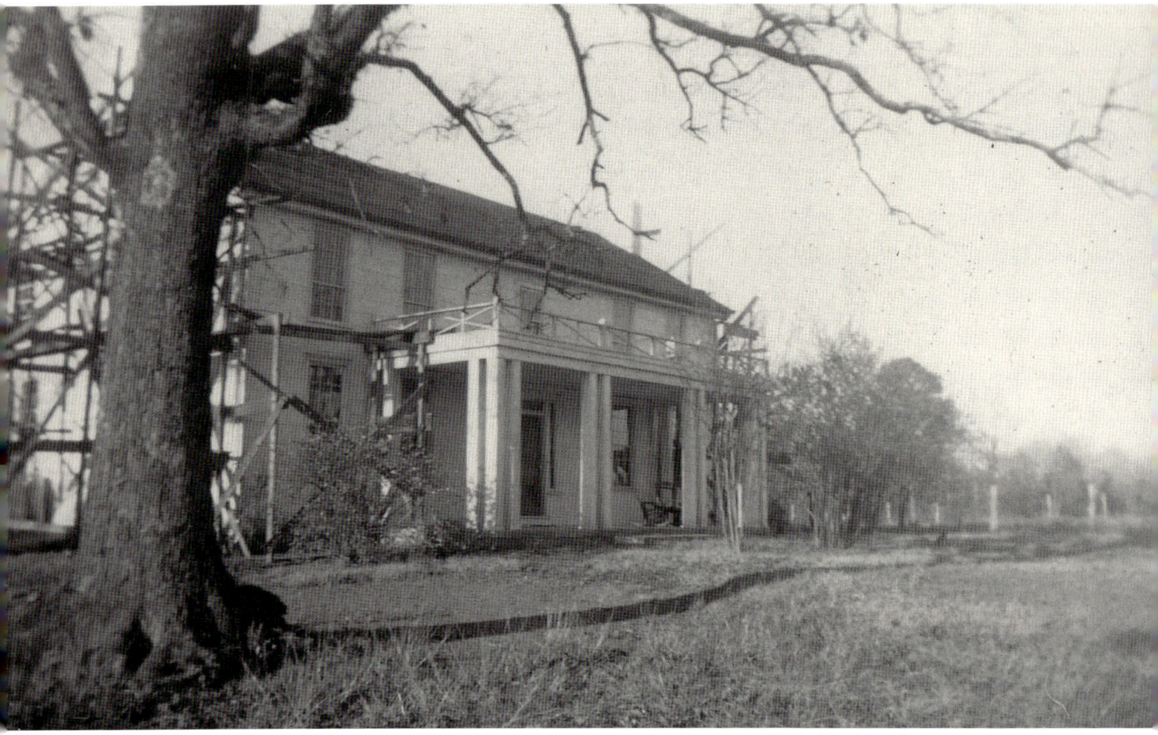

Originally owned by Rhoda Maroney, the property, which included over 800 acres, was purchased by Jacob and Nancy Perry around 1836. Devastated by the Civil War, Perry and subsequent generations resorted to selling vast tracts of land to stay financially afloat. In 1946, John Mahler purchased the home, Perry Hall, and the remaining 167 acres. For the Mahler family, the land produced a thriving cedar-harvesting operation. The family business shipped premium cedar timber using the local railroads.

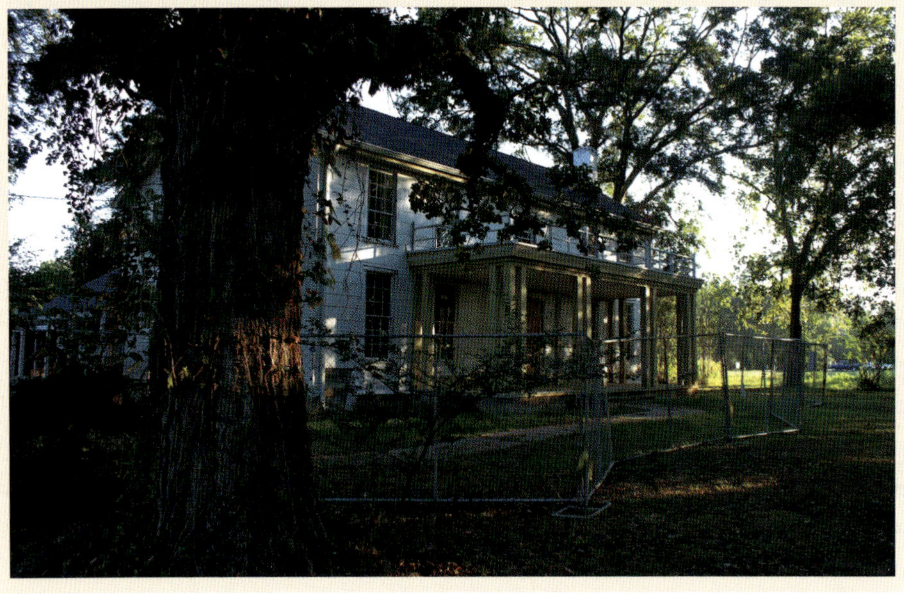

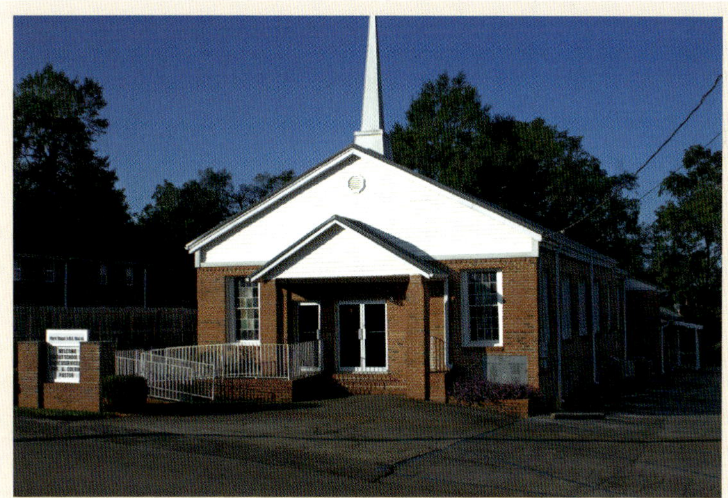

The city had a dynamic African American community known as Jacksonville a few blocks from downtown. A number of residents, including Jesse Brazier, helped found Ward Chapel African Methodist Episcopal Church in 1872, seen in this post–World War II image.

A thriving and dynamic church, Ward AME, and also Shiloh Missionary Baptist Church, served the African American community in Montevallo. For years, the nearby Shoal Creek offered a swimming hole for the segregated town. The current pastor is Alonzo Colvin.

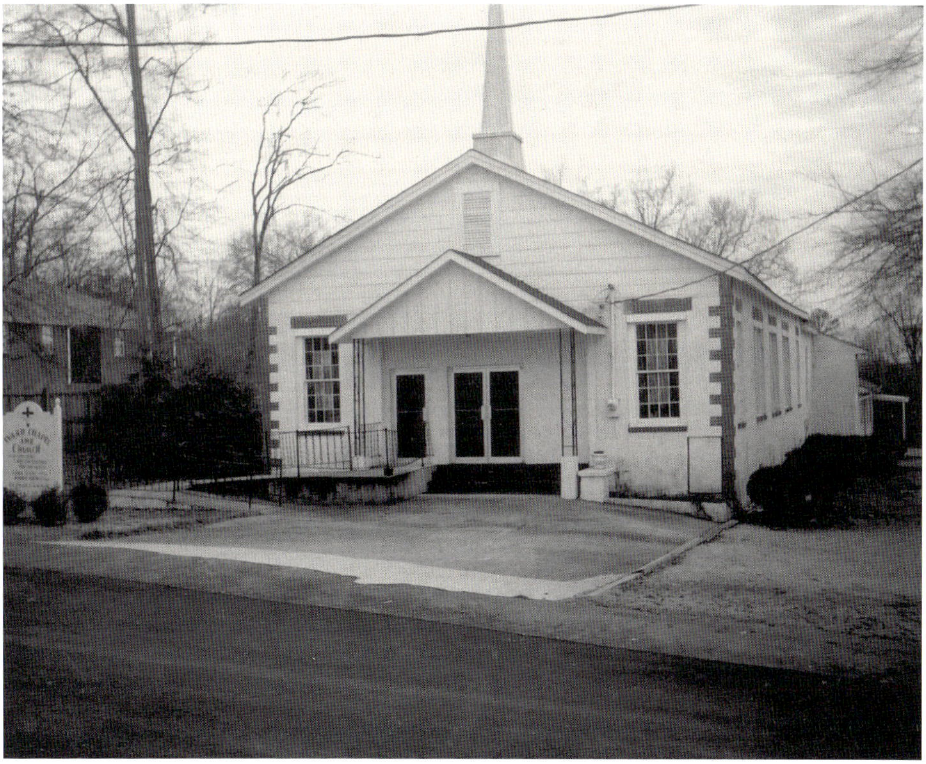

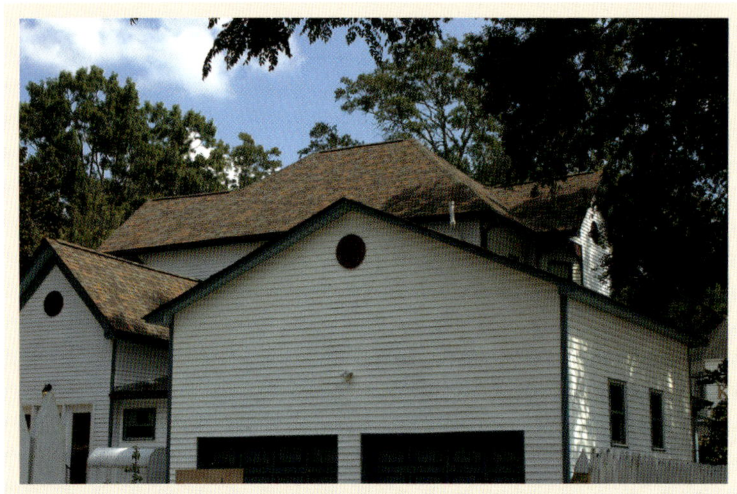

Dr. Edgar Gilmore Givhan purchased this Victorian Eastlake home shortly after its construction in 1880. His wife, Lena Peterson, was the daughter of the school's second president, Francis Peterson. Givhan served as the school's physician in the late 1890s before returning to private practice. Later owners Glenn and Doris "Dee" Lein possessed the home until her death in 2015. The home's current owners are restoring the residence to its authentic style. This c. 1910 photograph shows two younger Givhan family members.

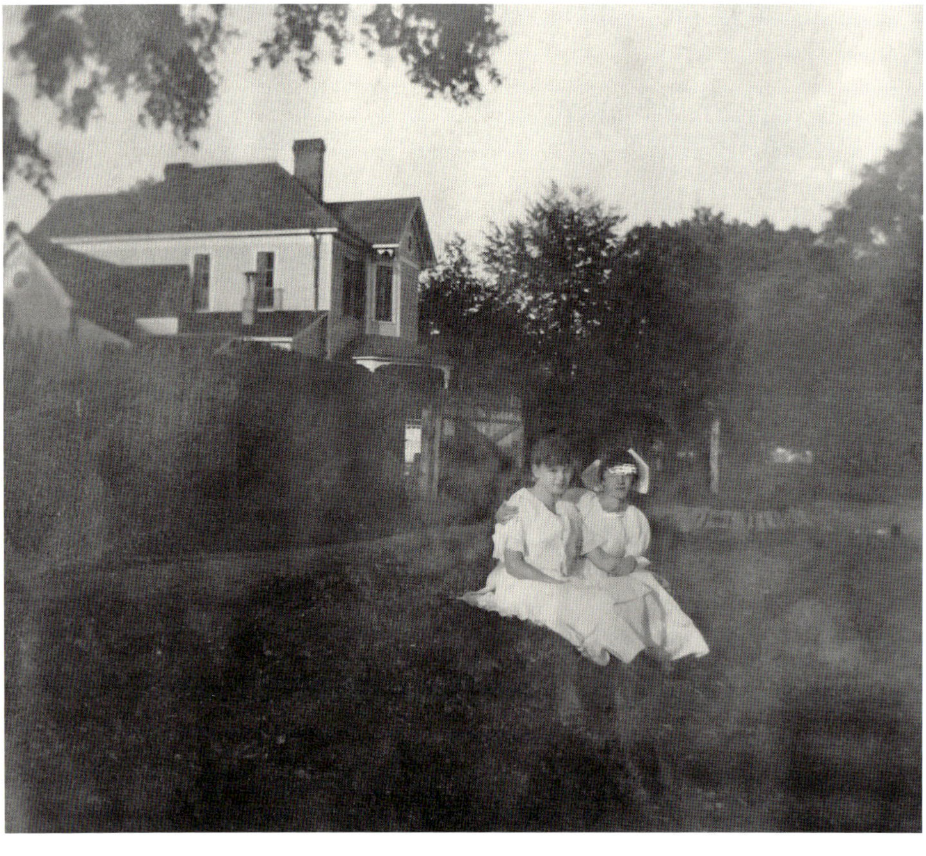

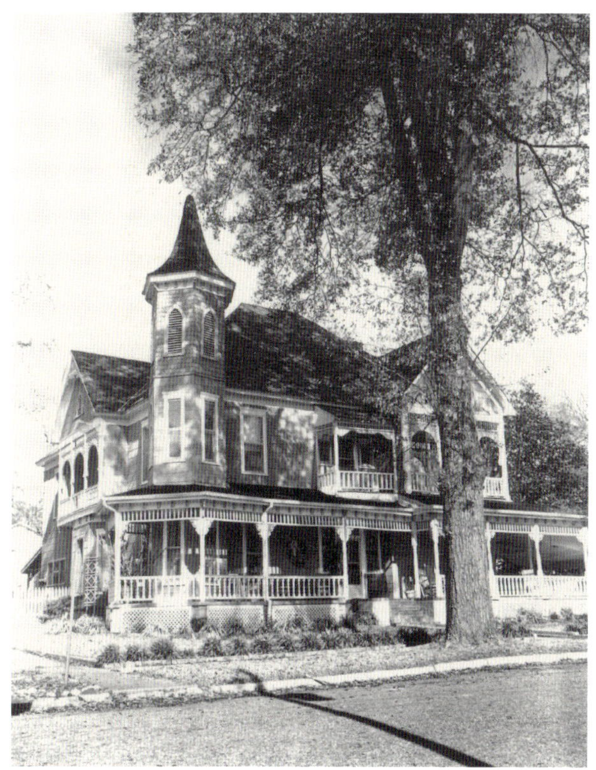

The McKibbon House (built in 1884) at 611 East Boundary Street is one of few Queen Anne–style Victorian homes to remain in Montevallo. For many years, it served as a bed-and-breakfast, though it is yet again today a private residence. Like several of the town's historic homes, it served an important role by providing lodging to travelers. The home earned a listing in the National Register of Historic Places in 2001 and has been restored to its past beauty.

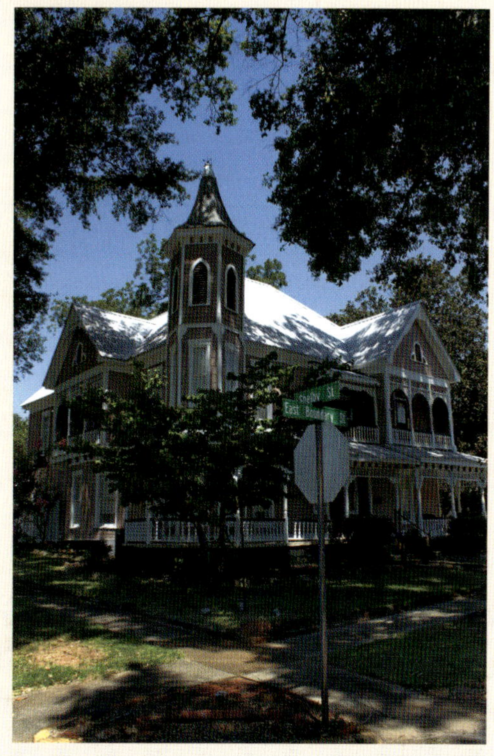

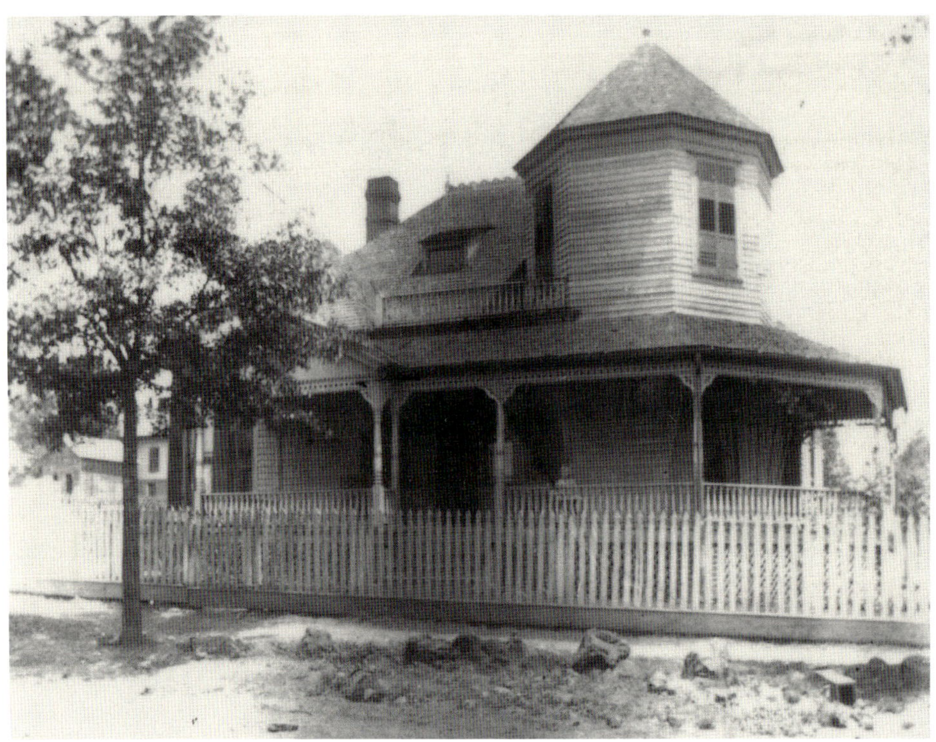

George Morgan, a dry goods store owner, built this two-story wood Victorian house in a simple Eastlake style in 1896. Morgan was also instrumental in the formation of Alabama College. In 1946, his son married Sarah Ruth Posey, who taught in the business administration department. Clyde and Sarah Adams Winslett were longtime owners of the house until her passing in 2015. Sarah Adams Winslett attended Alabama College. Today, the Morgan-Winslett Home hosts the Alpha Kappa Lamba fraternity.

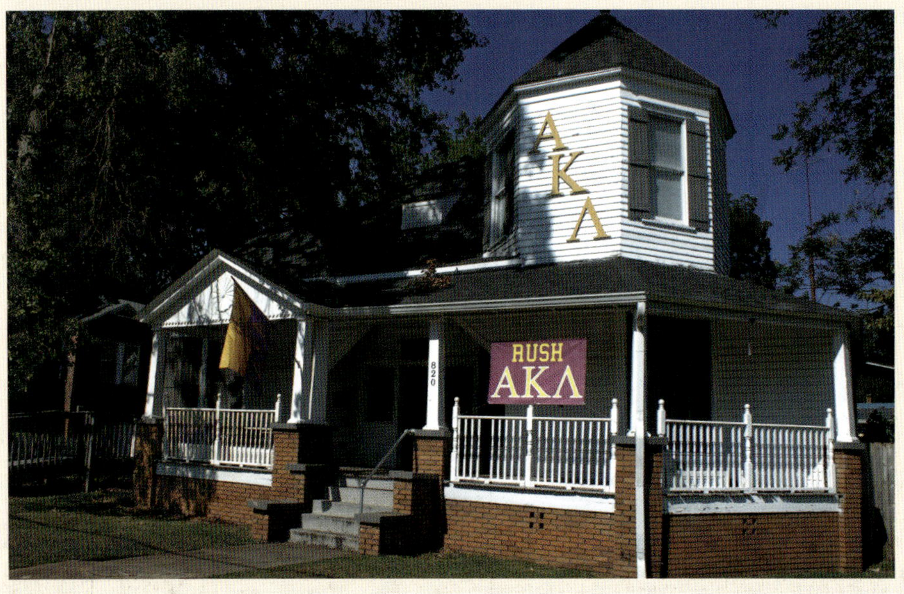

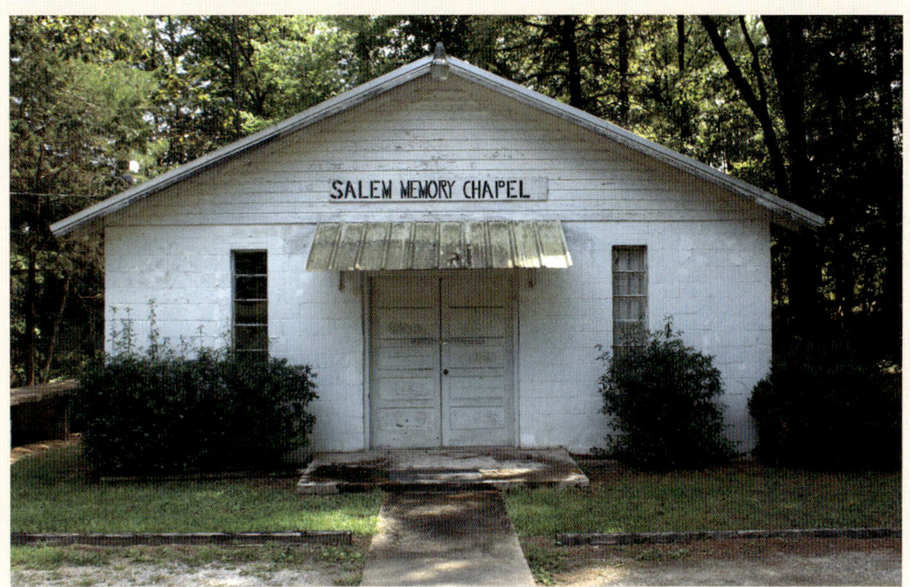

Starting in the late 1800s, Salem School operated as a one-room building for local farming families within walking distance. The school had a potbelly stove and educated students up to the sixth grade. The building closed in the 1940s, and in 1956, local parishioners built the Salem Memory Chapel, much out of materials from the Old Concord School in Dry Valley. The current site sits across Salem Road from Salem Cemetery, which has burials dating to the 1830s.

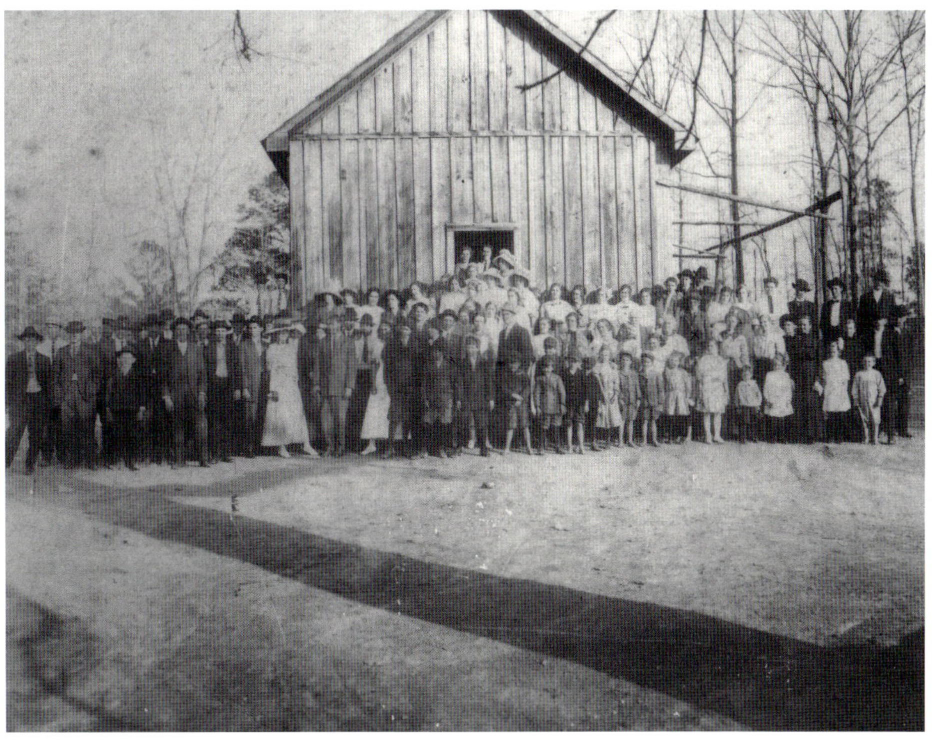

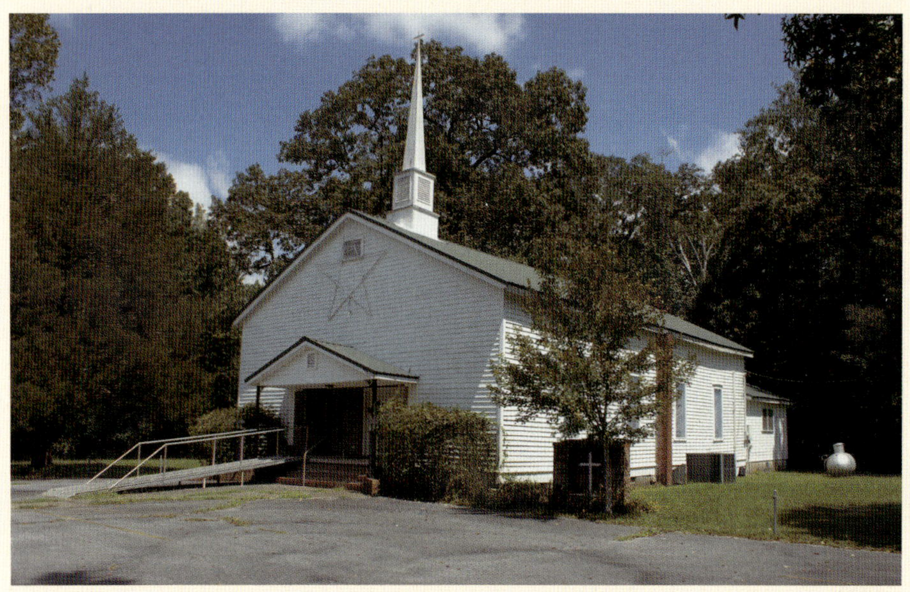

Built in 1891, Ebenezer United Methodist Church has long served the satellite community of Ebenezer, a few miles north of town. The church is named for Ebenezer Hern, who came to Alabama from Tennessee in 1818. Over the years, the church has seen numerous additions and improvements, including Sunday school rooms, electric lighting (installed in 1946), and a steeple dedicated in 1978 to Nathan Thomas Frost. This c. late-1980s photograph shows the church in a bucolic setting near Ebenezer Swamp.

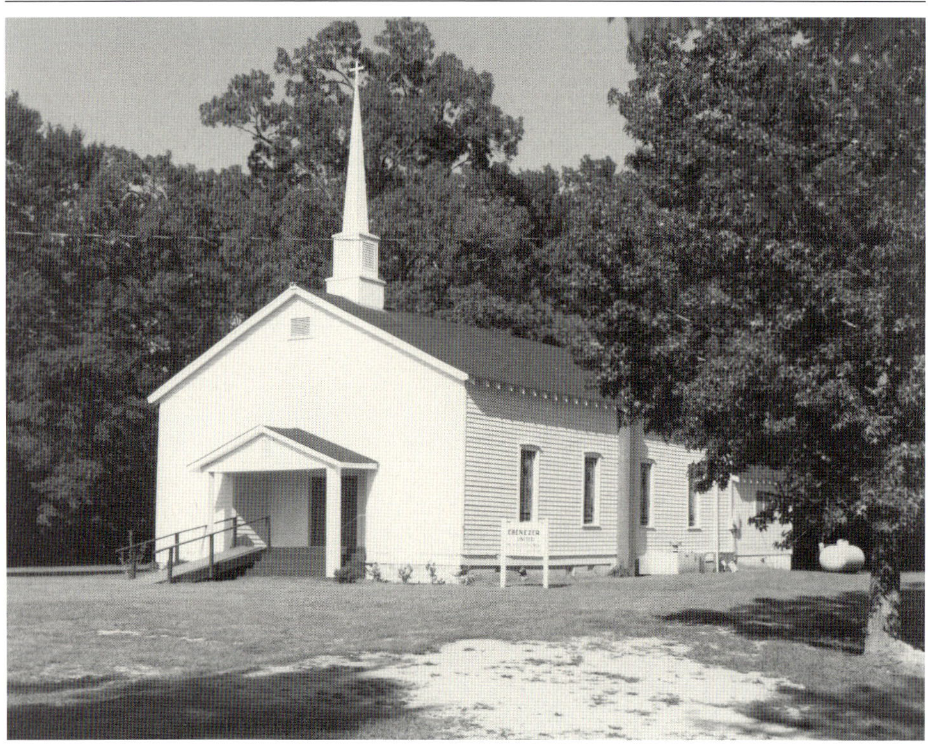

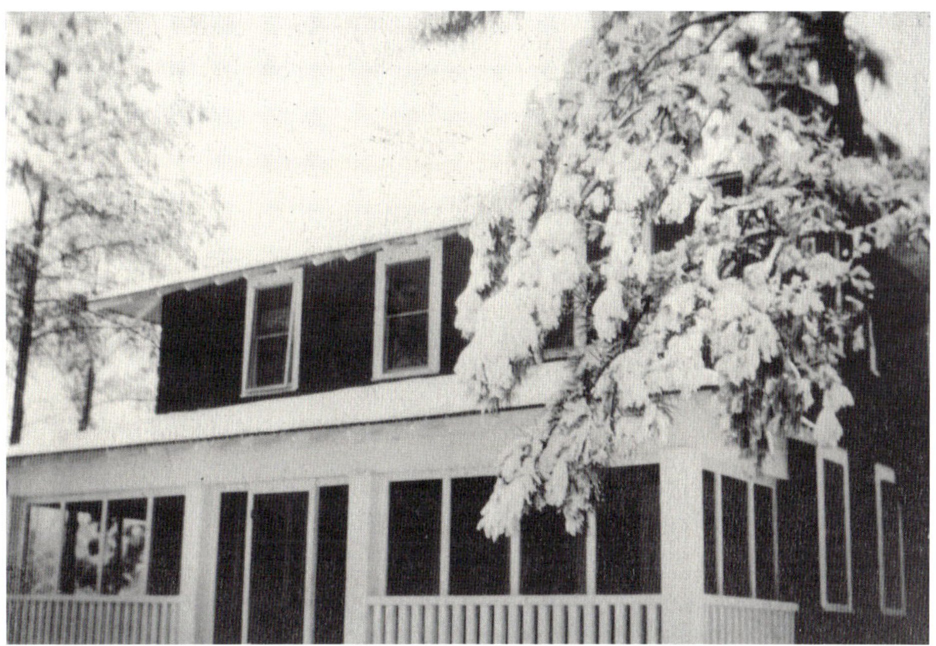

Louesa Jane Keys taught domestic science at the Alabama Girls Technical Institute between 1913 and 1917 and photographed structures on and off campus. One such building was a home of some 3,000 square feet, with a grand porch and a metal roof, nicknamed "Pinehurst," which sits at the corner of Highland Street and State Route 119. In the late 1930s, Reese Wooley, a prominent member of the community and US Navy veteran of World War II, lived here.

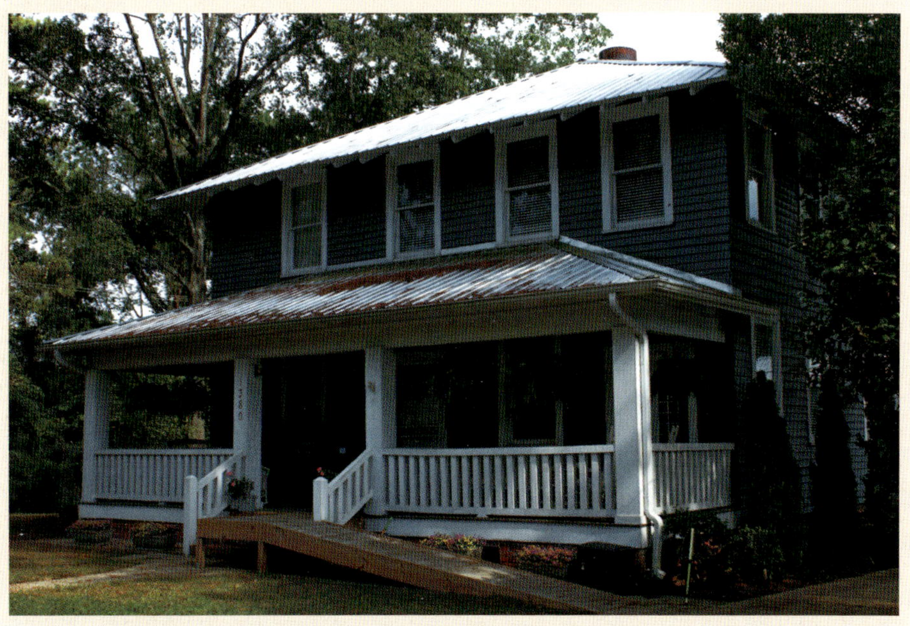

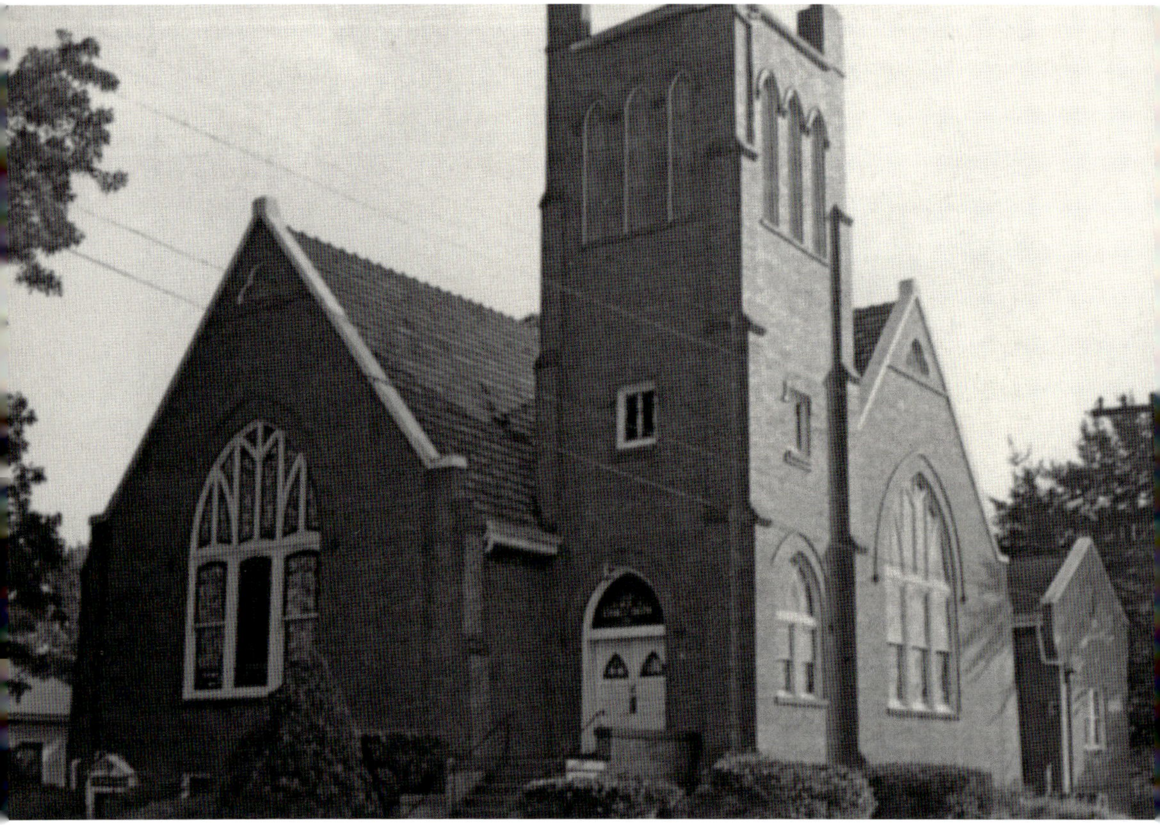

Montevallo's First United Methodist Church was organized in 1818. The original church was located near the current city cemetery site. When fire destroyed that church, the congregation moved services to the Masonic lodge. The next two subsequent church buildings were built on Island and Middle Streets, respectively, but fire and tornado destroyed them. The third structure served the congregation at that site until it purchased the current property in 1909.

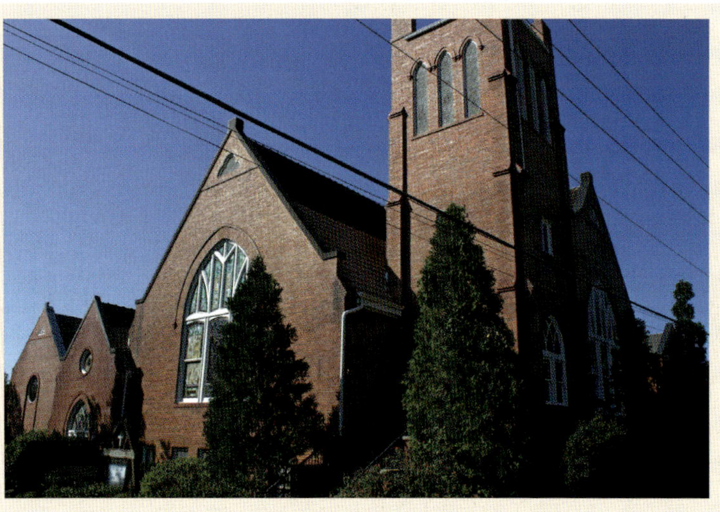

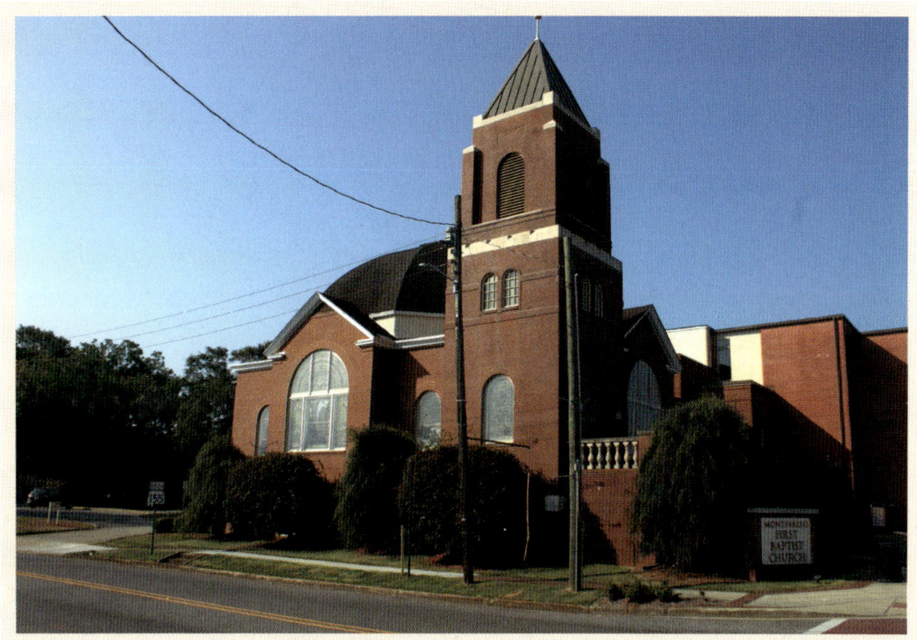

Baptists were represented among the first white settlers moving to the area in the early 1800s. The Montevallo First Baptist Church was formed in 1855 as a result of a split among the original Shoal Creek Baptist Church congregation. Town members located the new church on land donated by Edmund King, now the site of Main Hall. After a series of accidents and setbacks, the current brick church opened on Main Street in 1910 on land given by Henry Clay Reynolds.

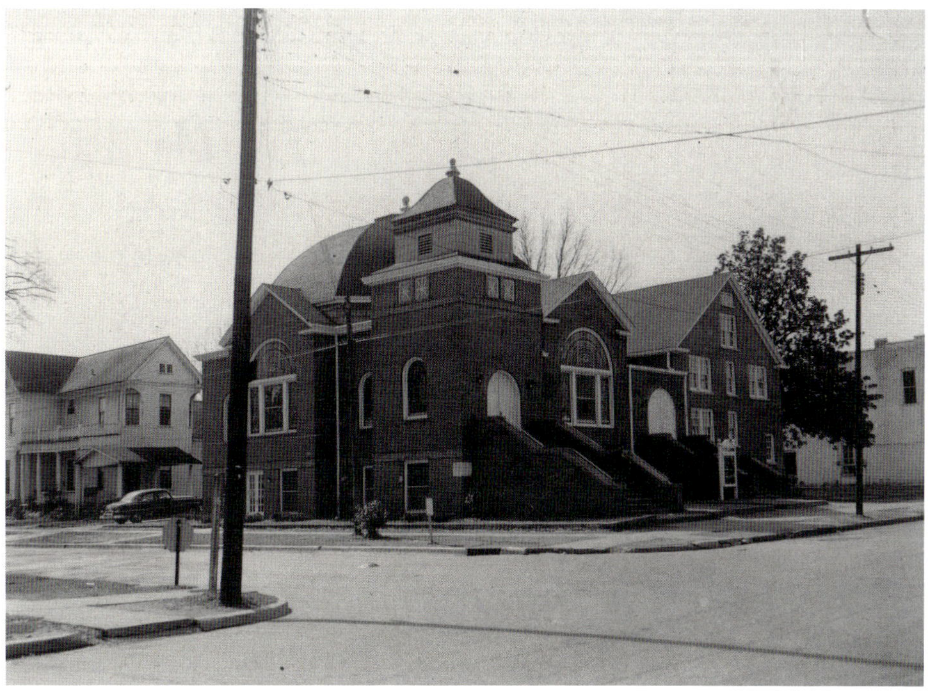

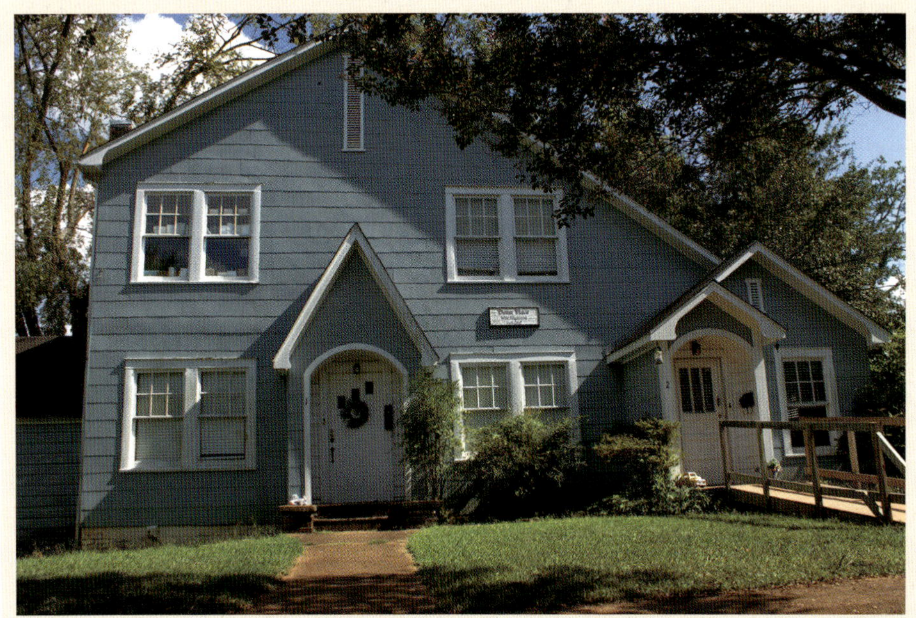

Alice Yeager operated a small photography studio in town in the early 1900s. Business success saw her expand and build this 1920s combination house and studio, a saltbox-inspired design with a catslide roof that cleverly integrated a carport. Yeager Studios was a longtime successful business well up to 1947. Later owners converted this campus-adjacent home into Dover Place Apartments, remodeling the carport into a second apartment. Mark Robinson currently owns this building.

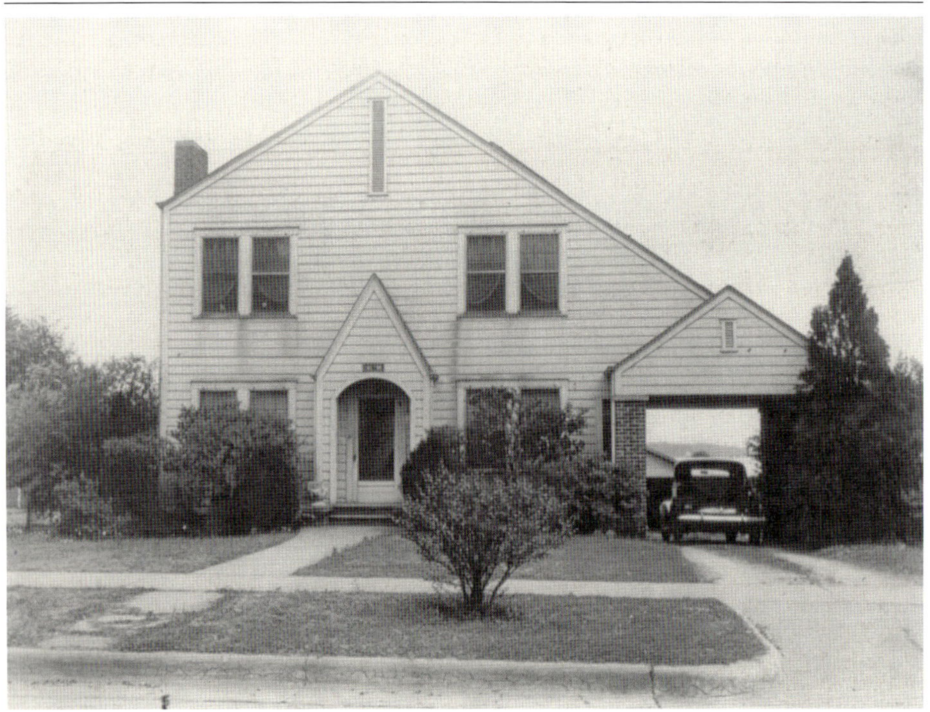

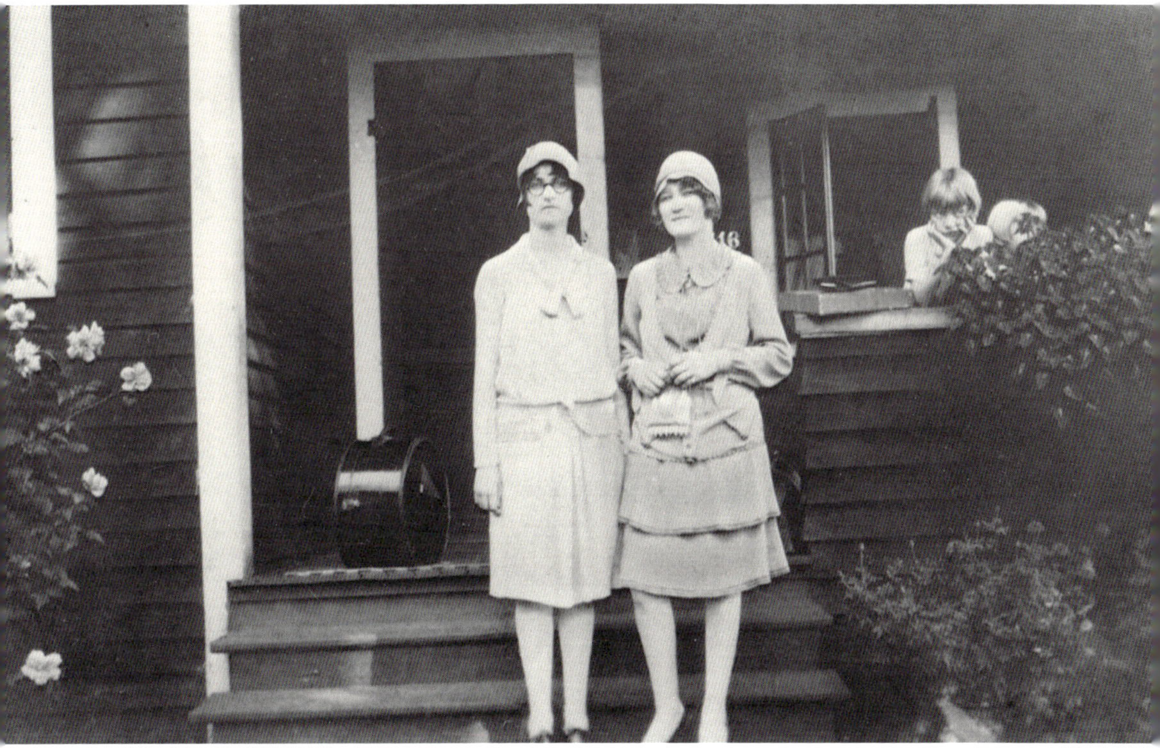

Missouri transplant Lucille Blanche Griffith, with a doctorate in history from Brown University, taught and researched at Alabama College from 1946 to 1973. During the latter part of her career, she served as Social Science department chair. Griffith edited several works and wrote a documentary history of Alabama as well as two campus histories. For many years, this home at Highland Street and Highway 119 served as her primary residence. (Past image courtesy of Meredith Tetloff.)

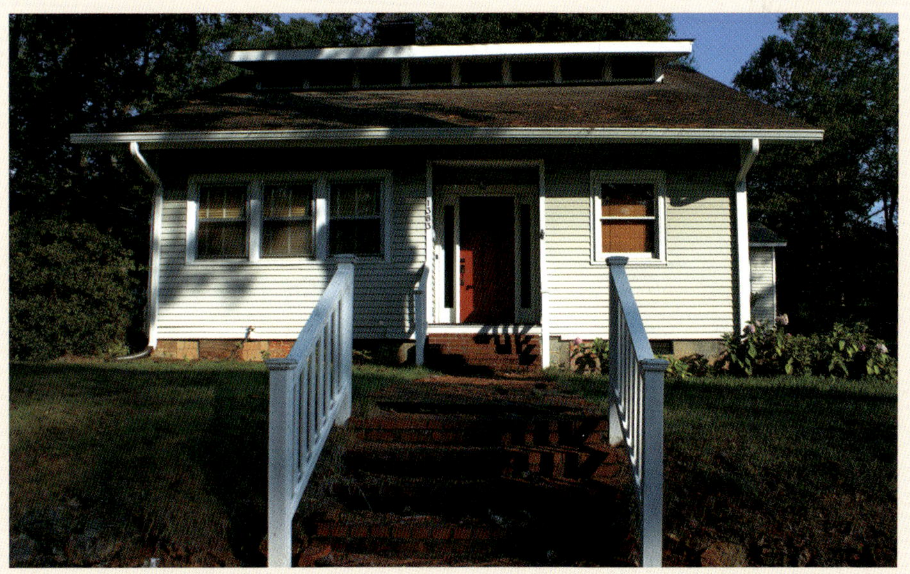

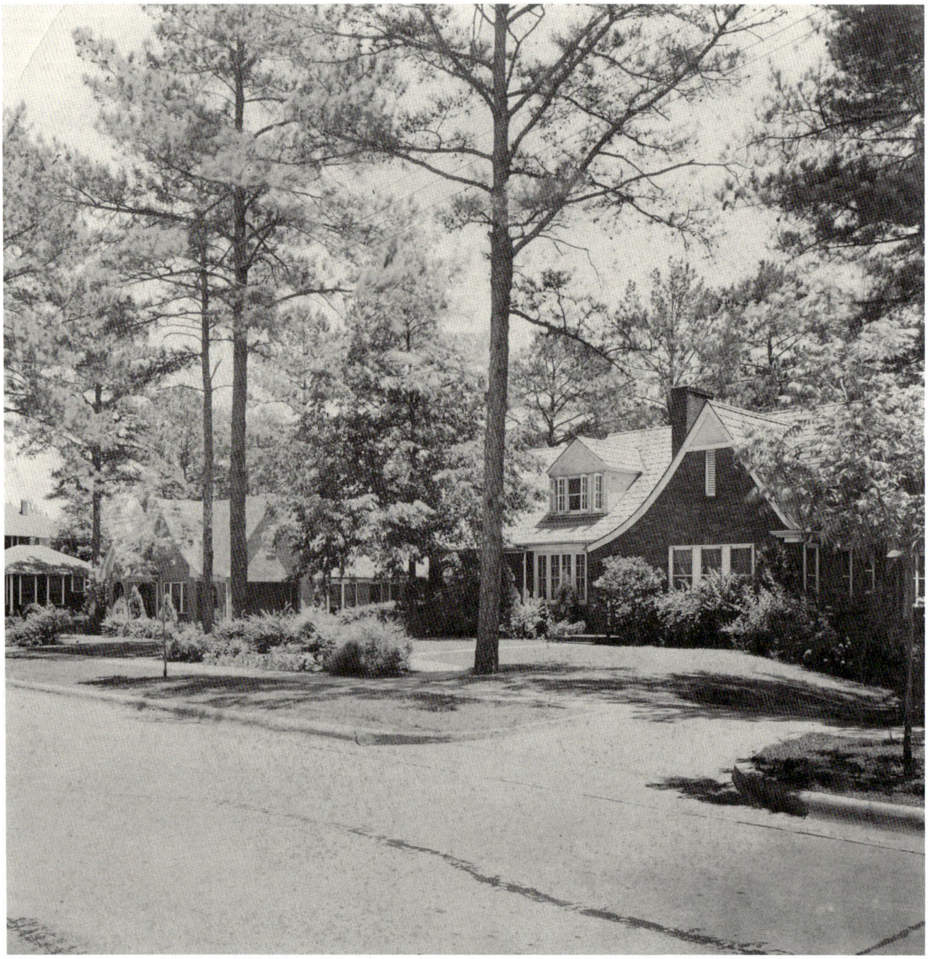

In 1940, Frances and Pete Givhan and Willilee and Walter Trumbauer lived in adjoining houses on Highland Avenue a few blocks from campus. Givhan served as mayor from 1940 to 1944 and also operated a Coca-Cola distribution business and an insurance agency. The Trumbauers (sometimes called Mr. and Mrs. "Trummie") were longtime and beloved faculty members at Alabama College in the English department. Walter turned his interest to theater and started a high school theater festival that later bore his name.

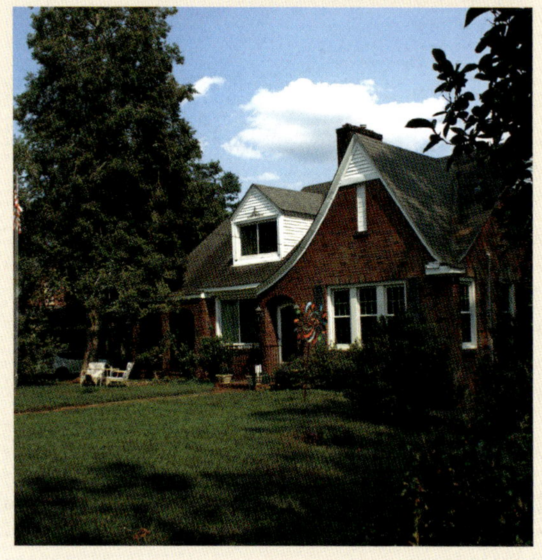

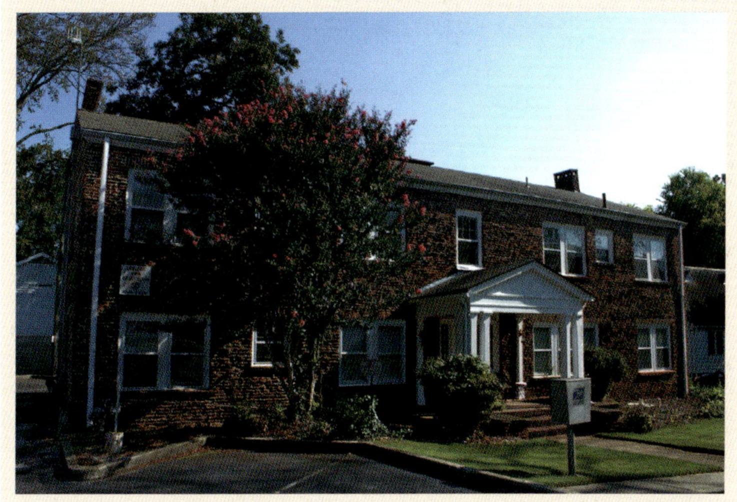

Just one block from campus, College View Apartments (built in 1928) features bleeding mortar brick joints and originally housed college faculty. It remains one of the oldest apartment buildings in the city. A whimsical 1938 article in the student newspaper, the *Alabamian*, headlines "College Professors Still Absent Minded at Montevallo," noting that four different faculty members gave four different names for the building. In 1988, after 60 years of existence, the owners remodeled the structure. Today, mostly university students live in the apartments.

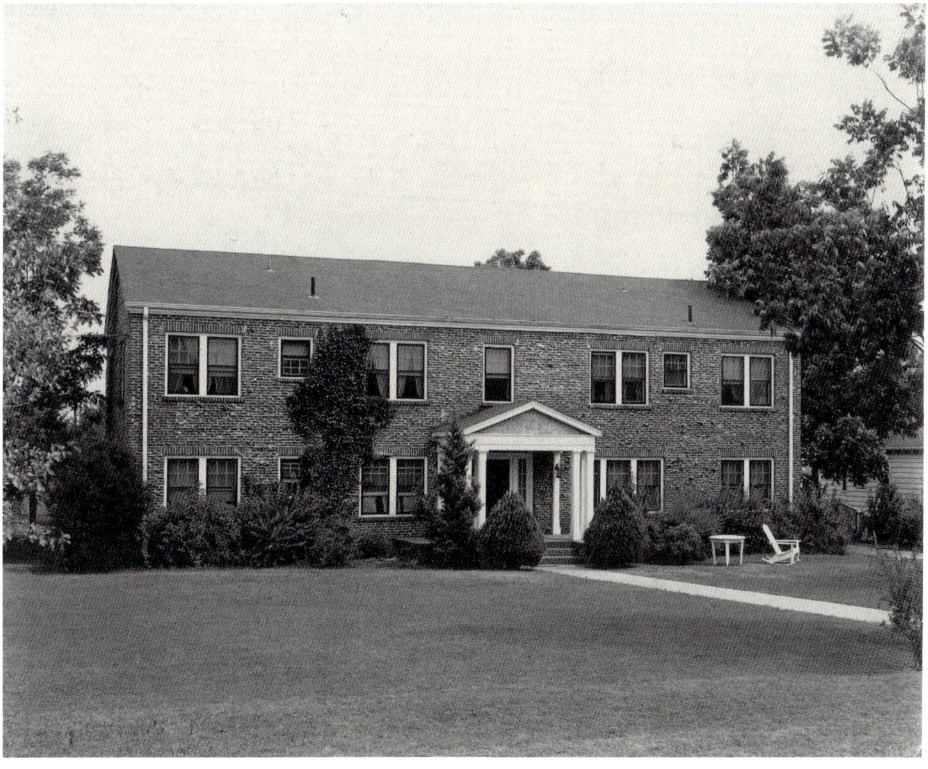